A COMPLETE GUIDE TO ESTABLISHING YOUR BUSINESS

# RESTAURANT BUSINESS

## START-UP GUIDE

# Paul Daniels

## Acknowledgements

Thanks to Jim Calkins who supported us with finance contributions. He has a way of explaining technical subjects that is easy to understand and comprehend. Thanks to Gary Thomas for his guiding thoughts and input about material dealing with leasing, and property management.

## Publisher's Note

Printed in The United States of America

Published by Venture Marketing

Daniels, Paul
*The Restaurant Business Start-up Guide*
Includes references and index.
ISBN-10: 1582911037
ISBN-13: 978-1582911038

Printing: 1582911037CS-1-2011
Updated: 2011

Design by Dan Titus. Edited by Marilyn Weishaar.

# Table of Contents

# Contents

## Chapter 2: Business Plan Primer

# Chapter 3: Financial Planning

# Contents

# Contents

## Chapter 5: Site Selection

## Chapter 6: Leases & Negotiation                         6.1

# Contents

# Contents

# Contents

# Introduction

The restaurant industry is the cornerstone of our nation's economy, career-and-employment opportunities, and community involvement — and its importance should continue to grow. Consider these statistics from the National Restaurant Association:

• Total restaurant industry sales were over $580 billion in 2010, represented by more than 945,000 locations.

• The overall economic impact of the restaurant industry is represented 49% of every food dollar spent.

• More than seven out of 10 eating-and-drinking places are single-unit (independent) operations.

• The average household expenditure for food away from home in 2008 was $2,698 More than seven out of 10 eating-and-drinking places are single-unit (independent) operations.

This is good news for anyone wishing to start a restaurant. However, all of this activity points to the increased need for organization. From the very beginning stages at start-up, right on through to the clang of silverware on opening day.

This book is designed to help you start a restaurant. I have concentrated on the start-up aspects rather than the operational day-to-day aspects of running a restaurant. For example, one of the key topics is how to develop your business plan. I have tried to include elements to address starting a store from scratch, and elements to buy an existing store.

It is assumed that you have basic computer skills, and that you can navigate your way around an IBM compatible system. This is important to get the most out of the Web site, and programs that go with this book.

## How to Use This Book

This book is designed to be used as an action plan for starting your restaurant. It is laid out in specific sections to attain this goal. Some of the chapters are grouped; others are specific to one particular topic. Therefore, you can skip around in this book rather than read it sequentially.

## Chapter 1: Preplanning

Chapter 1, *Preplanning,* is designed to expose you to a lot of information so that you will begin thinking about all the aspects that lie ahead. It asks many tough self-evaluation questions so that you will have a better understanding of your strengths and weaknesses. The chapter walks you through what will need to be accomplished in order to test the feasibility of your business idea. Explained are the different types of business entities, such as corporations and partnerships. The chapter basically acts as a large preplanning checklist that you can use to get started.

## Chapters 2 - 4: Business Plan Elements

Chapters 2 through 4 are grouped together. These are the chapters that explain what is needed to develop a detailed business plan and understand the financial information that will be required in the plan. Chapter 2, *The Business Plan Primer*, will introduce you to a business plan primer. I will go go over the basic elements needed to create a business plan and explain the primary points that need to be covered in each section of the plan.

Chapter 3, *Financial Planning,* introduces key elements of finance and what you will need to know in order to add some of these elements to your business plan. Jim Calkin is my mentor in this area. Much of the information in this part of the book is excerpted from Jim's book, *Business Buyers Handbook.* The perspective in this chapter is for buying an existing business.

Chapter 4, *The Business Plan*, is a sample plan that you can study to see how all the elements fit together. It is laid out following the outline presented in Chapter 2.

## Chapters 5 and 6: Location Elements

Chapter 5, *Site Selection*, is designed to educate you about the different locations for your store. Whether a shopping center or a shopping mall, it will explain what you need to know in order to select the best location for your business.

Location is key to the success in any retail operation. We will delve into the basics of site evaluation. We will also take a look at some leasing scenarios, so you can see first hand what to look for when negotiating your store lease.

Chapter 6, *Leases & Negotiation*, tells you about the main elements of commercial real estate leases, and what to look out for. It details percentage rent deals, per-square-foot rent, and many of the rent provisions, such as CAM, for which you will be responsible.

## Chapters 7 and 9: Build-out Elements

Chapter 7, *Design & Build-out*, takes you into the process of setting up your store. It explains what is required in regard to permits and licenses. Here you will find an explanation of the different space configurations that most landlords offer. Finally, there is a restaurant construction guide that outlines all construction requirements.

Chapter 8, *Equipment*, explains what you need to know about store equipment. Some of the topics include: Government regulations, sources for equipment, buying and leasing considerations, and equipment lease negotiations.

Chapter 9: *Financing Your Restaurant*, offers you a quick overview of some of the sources where you might find financing for your store. From partners, family, friends, government loan programs, to credit cards, this chapter offers strategies to help you get the necessary start-up capital.

## Chapter 10: Management & Operations

This chapter will introduce you to critical techniques that will help you with the the management of your store. I have concentrated on aspects that you will need to be familiar with before you open. Topics include: menu design, supplier selection and sourcing, hiring techniques, employee evaluation techniques, employee shift scheduling, and employee policies.

## Chapter 11: Safety

This chapter will explain some of the safety issues that you will need to be aware of. As the owner of a restaurant, you will need to pay special attention to the topics covered here. You will be shown how to develop programs for: food safety, employee injury prevention and fire safety.

## Chapter 12: Taxes, Permits & Insurance

This brief chapter will outline the most frequently asked questions about taxes, permits, and insurance.

## Chapter 13: The Web Site

Here you will find an overview of the Web site that is designed to go along with this book. Look for the Web Connect logo shown here, in the margins throughout this book. This will notify you about expanded chapter topics, Ebooks, or software that you can receive online. To register for the Web site, see Chapter 13.

## Appendix

In the appendix you will find reference material, such as bibliography and contact information.

## Final Notes

Throughout this book tips are offered and noted in the margins. Be sure to put your personal notes there too, as this will assist you with your critical thinking.

Again, in order to take full advantage of the software and spreadsheet templates that are at the Web site, it is assumed that you are able to use a computer, and the associated software for Internet access.

Finally, we hope that you find this book informative and hope it helps you with your business endeavors.

Good luck, and here's to your business success!

# Preplanning

This chapter is designed to get you thinking about the many aspects of your new business and what you will need to accomplish from a tactical point. It is designed to test the feasibility of your business idea. From evaluating yourself as an individual to providing detailed checklists, it will help you with preplanning. There are many questions asked and you will need to know the answers before you move forward with your endeavors. Use this chapter as a tool to honestly assess yourself.

The U.S. Small Business Administration (SBA) has compiled a going-into-business checklist, which is designed to help you stay on track. The checklist asks questions that can help reveal fail points in your thinking. Fail points are areas that can have negative consequences once you launch your company. If you can answer these questions thoroughly and positively, you will be prepared to begin the quest of starting your own business. If you stumble on these questions, you may have some more studying to do.

Successful businesses begin with a practical plan. Entrepreneurs need a solid background in the businesses they choose to launch.

The SBA correctly identifies these qualities for a successful start-up:

- A practical business plan - Although not a quality, it is critical to your success.
- The dedication and willingness to sacrifice to reach your goal.
- Technical skills (If you launch a trucking company, you better know about trucking.)
- Knowledge of management, finance, bookkeeping, and market analysis.

Clarify your reasons for launching, and even more importantly identify your strengths and weaknesses. Once you've answered these questions, you'll have a good idea whether you should launch right away, or hold off for awhile.

# Why Do You Want to Start Business?

As a first step, ask yourself why you want to start business. Identifying your reasons is important. People start a business for different reasons, including:

- Freedom from the daily work routine.
- Being your own boss.
- Doing what you want when you want to do it.
- Improving your standard of living.
- Freedom from a boring job.
- Having a product or service you believe will create a demand.

Some reasons are better than others. No reason is wrong; but be aware that there are tradeoffs. You can escape the daily routine of employment only to find that business ownership is more demanding. The checklist asks the difficult questions that can reveal holes in your thinking, that may have dire consequences once you launch your company.

# Self-Evaluation

### Do You Have What it Takes?

Going into business requires particular personal characteristics. This portion of the checklist explores your personal attributes. It is important to stay objective, and above all, be honest about your capabilities.

The goal here is to access your strengths and weakness, so you can develop a strategy to deal with those aspects of your new business that you will be directly involved with, and those that you will delegate to other parties. You may be great at finance and you may have the computer aptitude to develop your own menu artwork layout. However, you may not have the knowledge, or desire, to pursue all the marketing aspects of writing a business plan. Therefore, seek help in marketing.

### Personal Characteristics

- Are you a leader? Do others turn to you for help in making decisions?
- Do you make decisions easily?
- Do you enjoy competition?

• Do you have the required self-discipline?
• Do you usually plan ahead? Impulse is a dangerous trait in business owners.
• Do you like to meet new people?
• Do you get along well with a wide range of people?
• Can you delay gratification?

## Personal Conditions

This group of questions is vitally important for new business owners.

• Do you have the physical, emotional, and financial strength to launch a new company?
• Do you realize that running your own business may require working 12-16 hours a day, six days a week, even Sundays and holidays?
• Do you have the physical stamina to handle the workload and schedule?
• Do you have the emotional strength to withstand the strain of the disappointments and rejection that invariably come with launching a new enterprise?

## Consequences of Launching a Business

• Are you prepared to possibly lower your standard of living until your business is firmly established? It can take time to regain your standard of living if you quit a high-paying job.
• Is your family prepared to go along with the strains they also must bear? Launching without the support of family can kill a young business.
• Are you prepared to lose your savings? There's a reason they call it risk. Many people lose their entire investment.

You can escape the daily routine of employment only to find that business ownership is much more demanding.

Be ready to eat, drink, and sleep your new business. Like a newly planted plant, there will be a critical time while your business takes root.
Your time will be needed to develop systems that will help run the business. At the same time, you more than likely will be running the day-to-day operations.

## Your Business Knowledge

It is unlikely that you possess all of the particular skills and experience that are critical for business success. You'll need to learn as much as you can before starting your business.

- Have you ever worked in a managerial or supervisory capacity?
- Have you ever worked in a business similar to the one you want to start?
- Have you had any business classes in school?
- If you discover you don't have the basic skills needed for your business, will you be willing to delay your plans until you've acquired the necessary skills?

# Feasibility

Your business ideas and your market feasibility will become basic elements of your business plan. See chapters 2 and 4 for details about business plans. For now you can make a preliminary outline based on the following criteria. Briefly answer the questions the best that you can. The objective here is to test the feasibility of your business idea.

## Your Business Idea

Many entrepreneurs dive into business blinded by their dream before evaluating the potential of the business. Before you invest time, effort, and money, the following exercise will help you differentiate good ideas from those ideas destined to fail.

- Identify and briefly describe the business you plan to start.
- Identify the products or services you plan to sell.
- Does your product or service satisfy an unfilled need among potential customers you can reach?
- Can you make a profit? How long will it take to make a profit?
- Will your product or service be competitive based on quality, selection, price, or location?
- What will it cost to produce, advertise, sell & deliver?

## The Market

To succeed, you need to know who your customers are. To learn about your market, you need to analyze it. You don't have to be an expert market analyst to learn about your marketplace, nor does the analysis have to be costly. Analyzing your market is a way to gather facts about potential customers and a way to determine the demand for your products or services. The more information you have, the greater your chances of capturing a profitable segment of the market.

Sometimes the best market information is simply the knowledge you have gathered by being an enthusiast for the market: If you launch a taco stand, a lifelong interest in tacos helps. You can approach this several ways, however, it is critical to learn your market before investing time and money in an enterprise.

These questions will help you gather the information necessary to analyze your market and determine if your products or services will sell.

• Who are your customers and how often will they purchase your products?
• Do you understand their needs and desires?
• Do you know where they live and how to reach them?
• Will you offer the kind of products or services that are missing from the market but are likely to be valued?
• Will your product prices be competitive in quality and value?
• Do you know how to promote your products to your target customers?
• Do you understand how your business concept compares with competitors'?

Many entrepreneurs go into business blinded by dreams, unable to thoroughly evaluate its potential.

# Business Start-Up Planning

So far this checklist has helped you identify questions and problems you will face determining if your idea is feasible and converting your idea into reality. Through self-analysis you have learned your personal qualifications and deficiencies, and through market analysis you have learned if there is a demand for your product or service.

The following questions are grouped according to function. They are designed to help you prepare for opening day.

# Name and Legal Structure

- Have you chosen a name for your business? If so, will you want to trademark the name?
- Have you chosen to operate as a sole proprietorship, partnership, or corporation?

> **Choose a business.**
> **Choose a business name.**
> **Is the business legal?**

## Choosing a Business Structure

Once you decide to establish a business, a primary consideration is the type of business entity to form. Tax and liability issues, director and ownership concerns, as well as state and federal obligations pertaining to the type of entity should be considered when making your determination. Personal needs and the needs of your particular type of business should also be considered. The main types of business entities are:

- Sole proprietorship.
- Corporation.
- Limited liability company.
- Limited partnership.
- General partnership.
- Limited liability partnership.

## Sole Proprietorship

A Sole Proprietorship is set up to allow an individual to own and operate a business by him/herself. A Sole Proprietor has total control, receives all profits from and is responsible for taxes and liabilities of the business. If a Sole Proprietorship is formed with a name other than the individual's name (example: John's Fish & Chips), a fictitious business name statement must be filed with the county clerk or county recorder where the

*TIP*

**To Start a Sole Proprietorship:**

1. **File a Fictitious Name Statement** *(Also known as a DBA - Doing Business As) with the county recorder. This will notify all of your intent to establish a business under your new business name.*

2. **Advertise your DBA** *in a local paper. You must legally announce that you will be doing business under the fictitious name. Classified ads are fine.*

3. **Open a Bank Account:** *Take the DBA statement from the county recordor and your published ad to the bank to set up your bank account under your business name.*

principal place of business is located. No formation documents are required to be filed with the secretary of state. The secretary of state is the government agency that controls business entities. Other state filings may be required depending on the type of business and your regional location.

## Corporation

A Corporation is defined as a legal entity which separates the liability of the business from that of the owner(s). In other words, the owner(s) of a Corporation cannot be held personally liable for lawsuits filed against the business, and the owner(s) credit cannot be affected by the business debts.

*Why Incorporate?*

Protection is the chief reason for incorporating. Many people believe that their businesses are too small or too new to incorporate. Others believe that to incorporate would be too expensive. Nothing can be farther from the truth. Here are some benefits of incorporating:

• Provides lawsuit and asset protection.
• Provides tax advantages not available to individuals who obtain businesses or partnerships.
• Avoids personal liability.
• Establishes lines of credit, which are not available to individuals and partnerships.
• Provides easy way to capitalize your business.
• Offers capital for operating expenses.

## Limited Liability Company

A Limited Liability Company generally offers liability protection similar to that of a corporation but is taxed differently. Limited Liability Companies may be managed by one or more members. In addition to filing the applicable documents with the secretary of state, an operating agreement among the members as to the affairs of the Limited Liability Company and the conduct of its business affairs is required.

*TIP*
*Nevada and Wyoming corporations have become popular over the past several years because they offer privacy and lower operating costs than offered by many states.*

### Limited Partnership

A Limited Partnership may provide limited liability for some partners. There must be at least one general partner that acts as the controlling partner while the liability of limited partners is normally limited to the amount of control or participation they have engaged in. General partners of a limited partnership have unlimited personal liability for the partnership's debts and obligation.

### General Partnership

A General Partnership must have two or more persons engaged in a business for profit. Except as otherwise provided by law, all partners are liable jointly for all obligations of the partnership unless agreed by the claimant. Profits are taxed as personal income for the partners. Filing at the state level is optional.

### Limited Liability Partnership

A Limited Liability Partnership is a partnership that engages in the practice of public accountancy, the practice of law, or the practice of architecture, or services related to accountancy or law. A Limited Liability Partnership is required to maintain certain levels of insurance as required by law.

## Your Business and the Law

A person in business is not expected to be a lawyer, but each business owner should have a basic knowledge of laws affecting the business. Here are some of the legal matters you need to be acquainted with. Also, you will find checklists, which are broken out by sections.

• Do you know which licenses and permits you may need?
• Do you know the business laws you will have to obey?
• Do you have a lawyer who can advise you and help you with legal papers?
• Are you aware of Occupational Safety and Health Administration (OSHA) requirements?

Do you know about:

• Regulations covering hazardous material?
• Local ordinances covering signs, snow removal, etc.?
• Federal tax code provisions pertaining to small business?
• Federal regulations on withholding taxes and Social Security?
• State workers' compensation laws?

When starting a new business, there are many important decisions to make and many rules and procedures that must be addressed. While there is no single source for all filing requirements, the following checklists have been developed to assist you in starting your business.

## Checklists

### Federal Government

• Register or reserve federal trademark/service mark.
• Apply for patent if you will be marketing an invention.
• Register copyrights.
• Contact the Internal Revenue Service for information on filing your federal tax schedules.
• Apply for employee identification number with the Employment Department if you will have employees.
• Check compliance with federal wage laws.

## State Government

- File partnership, corporate or limited liability company papers with the secretary of state's office.
- File state tax forms with the franchise tax board.
- Find out about workers' compensation if you will have employees.
- Apply for sales tax number with the board of equalization if needed.
- Check state wage law.
- Observe OSHA safety compliance.
- Draft fire egress plan.
- Develop injury and illness prevention program.
- Check compliance with health laws.

## Local Government

- Get any required business licenses or permits.
- Order required notices (advertisements you have to place) of your intent to do business in the community. File DBA, (Doing Business As).
- Get local building permit from building department.
- Fire permits - You must pass fire safety inspection. Have fire extinguishes? Fire sprinkler system in place? Note: Periodic fire safety inspections will be required after opening.
- Check zoning laws.

## Protecting Your Business

It is becoming increasingly important that attention be given to security and insurance protection for your business. There are several areas that should be covered. Have you examined the following categories of risk protection?

- Fire.
- Theft.
- Robbery.
- Burglary.
- Vandalism.
- Accident liability.

## Landlord Demands

Your landlord will require that you carry insurance to protect his/her interests. In addition to the categories mentioned above, for example, they may insist that you carry liability specifically for the large plateglass windows, which are found in most shopping centers these days. *See chapter 6, Leases & Negotiation and the sample lease included there for more details.*

## Other Tasks

- Open a bank account for the business.
- Have menus, business cards, and stationery printed.
- Purchase equipment or supplies.
- Order inventory, signage, and fixtures.
- Get an email address.
- Find a Web hosting company.
- Get your Web site set up.
- Have sales literature prepared.
- Call everyone you know and let them know you are in business.
- Advertise in newspapers or other media if yours is the type of business that will benefit from paid advertising.
- Call for information about Yellow Pages advertising.
- Have business phone or extra residential phone lines installed.
- See if the business name is available for use as a domain name.
- Register the domain name even if you aren't ready to use it.
- Install alarm system.
- If you plan to accept credit cards and bank debit cards, you will need to set up a credit card processing system.

Discuss the types of coverage you will need and make a careful comparison of the rates and coverage with several insurance agents before making a final decision.

## Business Records

- Are you prepared to maintain complete records of sales, income and expenses, and accounts payable and receivable?
- Have you determined how to handle payroll records, tax reports, and payments?
- Do you know what financial reports should be prepared and how to prepare them?

## Suppliers

- Have you made a merchandise plan based upon estimated sales to determine the amount of inventory you will need to control purchases?
- Have you found reliable suppliers or employees who will assist you in the start-up?
- Have you compared the prices, quality, and credit terms of suppliers?

# Business Plan Primer

*Avoid a crash: Plan!*

This chapter presents an overview of the basic elements of a business plan. The outline explained here serves as a template for the sample business plan in chapter 4. Study this chapter and then turn to chapter 4 to see how the basic elements of the plan are developed. This chapter also includes information about how to develop your marketing plan, which is part of the business plan.

If you are unfamiliar with financial reports, you might want to jump to chapter 3, *Financial Planning*, at this point in order to become familiar with the financial elements presented in this chapter.

# Business Plan Structure

1. Summary.
2. Body.
3. Conclusion.

## Executive Summary

This should be an overview and lead-in to the rest of the business plan. It is a summary of the main topics within the business plan. It should emphasize your competence in three key areas: Marketing, technical capabilities, and financial management.

### The Business Concept

Describe your product or service. Where possible, supplement with diagrams, illustrations or pictures in the final package you show to prospective lenders or investors. This information can be referenced in an appendix.

### Marketing Approach

Provide a brief description of your market strategy and the market segment you will be trying to reach. Outline the channel(s) you will use to reach this market, such as direct mail, retail, or wholesale distributors.

### Financial Features

Provide estimated dollar amount of sales and net profits that you project for each of the first 3 to 5 years of operation, then set forth the amount of starting capital you will need. Where cash flow is negative (as is usual) in the first few years, it may be helpful to show your net cash exposure or cumulative negative cash flow for each month or quarter, to show that your initial starting capital will be more than sufficient to cover such maximum exposure.

### Start-up Costs

Provide a brief overview of the start-up costs. This is basically a digest of the pro forma financial information that you will prepare.

## Current Business Position

Provide pertinent information about the company, and whether or not it is a start-up venture: How long it has been in operation. The form of the business: proprietorship, partnership, or corporation.

## Achievements to Date

Give an overview detailing any major achievements since the company opened. Provide examples of patents and prototypes. Also, mention where your facility is located. If you are a start-up venture, mention any of the relevant points mentioned above and/or where you currently are in your planning.

## Statement of Objectives

Sell your proposal to prospective investors, discussing the unique advantages your product or service has over existing products and services. State both your short-term and long-term business objectives for the business, and describe the image you want to create for your product or firm.

## Qualifications of Principals

Provide your background qualifications to run this particular business, citing education, overall business experience and particularly any successful experience in a closely related type of business operation. Also describe, if applicable, the qualifications of your partners or other co-owners who will be part of the management (or board of directors, in the case of a corporation) of your proposed business.

## Background of Proposed Business

Spell out the background conditions in the business in question, including how, where, and when the product is being used, as well as where trends in the business or industry seem to be leading. Also, discuss the main players (i.e., your competitors), or likely competitors, if the venture is a start-up operation. Explain where your business will fit in this picture. Will you be on the cutting edge of what is happening, or just one of the pack that is not in the same league as the leaders? If it is the latter, you will need a very convincing rationale to show why you can garner enough business to meet your financial objectives.

## Product Use

Provide a complete detailed technical description of the product or service to be offered, including a summary of any test data. Describe any tests that are currently planned. Show that you are anticipating the future by outlining any further refinements or logical next steps for developing an improved or different product later (or comparable plans for further innovations in a service business). This is your chance to show that what you have is a better mousetrap and is also technically feasible.

## Industry Overview and Trends

Provide an overview of your industry. Detail any discussions that provide simple graphical representations of the current situation in your industry. Mention any trends that are evident in your industry and/or regarding your products. Through research you can analyze your restaurant market and market potential, helping you make informed decisions.

Information for this part of the business plan is available from two sources:

• Primary research - Collecting the data and compiling it yourself.
• Secondary research - Obtaining the information from already published sources.

## Strength and Weakness Analysis

This is where you will do your competitive analysis. Prepare a weighting-scoring model in order to evaluate your key competitors. Primary competitors are in the same business that you are such as, hamburger stands. Secondary competitors would be all other restaurants in your immediate target area. The goal is to rank your business in relation to your competition.

When you know how you rank in relation to your competition, you then can form plans and contingency plans to deal with them.

Basically, the model allows an objective overview of subjective information. It allows you to weight specific criteria - or rank the importance of criteria. Score the criteria, then, total the scores.

To learn how to develop a weighting-scoring model, see chapter 10, *Management & Operations.*

## Marketing Strategy and Plan

Discuss here your marketing plan or strategy. This will include identifying the market segment you are seeking to reach, and the various means through which you intend to reach it, such as door-to-door sales, retail sales, direct mail, media advertising, selling through sales reps, jobbers, or multi-level distributorships, or whatever else you plan to do. If you can, mention the degree of market penetration and market share you expect to achieve, year by year, for the period for which the business plan is making projections (say 3 to 5 years). Create a budget for all the associated costs and include this in the business plan.

### Market Strategy

Are you the market leader in your industry? Challenger? Do you plan to use a nicher strategy and deal with segments of the industry currently being ignored?

Give a detailed account of what strategy you will use and how you will implement it. The following is an overview of basic market strategies.

# Overview of Market Strategies

## Market Leaders

The market leader is the main player in any market with the most market share - the biggest piece of the total pie. For example, Coca-Cola Company is the market leader in the soft-drink industry and McDonalds is the leader in the fast-food market. The primary objective of dominant players is to remain number one. This objective may be accomplished through:

### 1. Expanding of the total market size.

- **New users** - Target customers outside of primary market segment.
- **New uses** - Kiosk food service, cart food service.
- **More usage** - Frequent visitor promotions.

### 2. Protecting current market share.

- **Innovation strategy** - Introduces new product ideas. Is the leader in promotional strategies. Takes the offensive against all competitors.
- **Confrontation Strategy** - Price war, promotional war. Success through intimidation.
- **Harassment Strategy** - Hire away key people, bad mouth, apply political pressure, and other illegal or unethical practices. Under the table hardball.

### 3. Expanding its present share of the market.

Profitability tends to increase with market share. It is better to have 90% of the 10%. A difference of 10% in market share may be accomplished by a difference of about 5 points in pre-tax return on investment (ROI). Businesses with market shares above 40% earn an average ROI of 30%, approximately three times that of firms with shares under 10%.

However it is expensive for the dominant firm to increase market share in a market where it is already the clear leader. Furthermore, other competitors in the market will fight harder if they are facing a diminishing market share.

## Market Challengers

Market challengers are firms that occupy the second, third, or fourth place in an industry. They are "runner-up" companies. Examples include: Pepsi Cola Company and Wendy's Restaurants. Runner-up firms must attack the leader or another runner up firm if they are to increase market share. The market challenger has three basic strategic alternatives:

1. **Direct Attack** - They can go right for the leader, perhaps with direct product discounts or with a promotional campaign.

2. **Back-door or Blindside Strategy** - Basically the challenger "runs" around the dominant firm rather than attacking it directly. For example, the challenger specializes in tight retail markets that the leader will ignore because the region doesn't meet its traffic requirements.

3. **Guppy Strategy** - Attack a smaller competitor and obtain market share at its expense, rather than taking on the market leader. If a smaller restaurant goes out of business, then market share can be increased.

Within each of these strategic alternatives the market challenger has a number of tactical alternatives:

- Discounting Price - Equal value but lower price. Example: Sizzler restaurants.
- Lower quality - Lower quality of service but much lower price. Example: Fast-food restaurants.
- Prestige - Higher quality, higher price. Example: Jamba Juice pricing.
- Concentration - Greater concentration of stores by fewer markets served. Example: Many fast-food players.
- Improved Service - For example: McDonalds, "We'll serve you in less than a minute, or it's free."
- Distribution Innovation - Develop a new channel of distribution. Example: Starbucks retailing of ice-cream and bulk coffees through grocery stores.
- Cost Reduction - Maintain lowest cost structure in industry. Example: Reduce overhead.
- Intensive Promotion - Similar to price war but with advertising and sales blitzes as the primary focus.

## Market Nichers

Almost every industry includes a number of minor firms that operate in some segment of the market to avoid clashing with its larger competitors. An example is Shasta Cola and private label colas found at local grocery stores. New restaurants especially must find such a niche. The ideal market niche would have the following characteristics:

- Profitable size.
- Growth potential.
- Neglected by major chains.
- Defendable against major chains.

Some examples of how a new restaurant can be successful as a market nicher are:

- Locate in underserved markets - Inner city.
- Specialize on specific segment - Airline catering, hospital commissary.
- Focus on one market segment - College foodservice.
- Customized service - Unique self-service delivery systems.
- Service features - Better trained servers, valet parking.
- Unique location - Mountain biking route; sports oriented areas.
- Usage Segmentation - Based on light users versus heavy users. This is an example of the 80/20 rule of business, whereby 80% of business will come from 20% of the customers. The goal is to find the other 20%. In the case of your restaurant, find the 20% that are not repeat customers of established businesses. Then, address this population with a promotional campaign.

The market nicher is a practitioner of the concept of market segmentation, utilizing multiple dimensions in the delineation of markets.

# The Four Ps of Marketing

## Product

Give a detailed overview of your product(s) and/or service(s). Include any factors that make it different and why these factors are an advantage to your competitors' product. That will differentiate you in the market place. Illustrate your menu offerings. Define all your products.

## Place

Describe how you will distribute your product or service in the market. Will you reach your target audience by door-to-door sales, retail sales, direct mail, media advertising, selling through sales reps, jobbers, or multi-level distributorships? Describe your plant or store location. For example, your restaurant may be located in a retail shopping center. For more details on locations see chapter 5, *Site Selection*.

## Pricing

Describe how you will price your product or service.

Will you use penetration pricing to gain market share or will you price your product as a prestige product, charging a higher price? Are you the only one on the block with this type or product/service? Explain how you arrived at your pricing.

For example, when you are operating your new store, you might use penetration pricing to drive out a smaller competitor. This "low-ball" pricing strategy can work fine as long as you can still cover your overhead costs. This type of pricing is usually used to increase market share.

Prestige pricing is used when you want to charge a high price for a high-quality product. Fine dining restaurants follow this structure.

Markup pricing is the most popular method used by wholesalers and retailers in establishing a sales price. When the merchandise is received, the retailer adds a certain percentage to the figure to arrive at the retail price. An item that costs $1.80 and is sold for $2.20 carries a markup of $0.40, or 18% of the retail price. The initial markup is also referred to as the "Mark-on".

Pricing to the competition can be done if it covers your operation costs and still makes a profit. Formula pricing is similar to markup pricing. A fixed value is multiplied by the cost. For example, a restaurant might charge five times the cost for a meal product: 5 x $0.85 = $4.25 selling price.

Psychological pricing is a method to persuade a customer to buy. For example a price of $2.99 for a "value" meal may appeal to a customer who is looking for a discount meal. By charging $2.99 rather than $3.00, the customer perceives value in the product because of the "odd numbered" price. Discount stores and fast-food restaurants use this pricing in conjunction with their primary pricing scheme.

## Promotion

How will you promote your product? Discuss in this segment how you plan to go about creating an awareness of the product among its ultimate consumers, through advertising, publicity or otherwise, even though most of your sales may be made to middlemen such as wholesalers or retailers.

Cover all methods you will employ, such as telemarketing, circulars, print or electronic media advertising, direct mail, catalogs, or other means. Here it will be useful to include menus, photocopies of dummy ads, brochures or other promotional materials that you may have already prepared, if you feel they will be effective in selling your business plan.

## Market Segmentation

Market segmentation is the process of dividing a market into specific differentiated segments that have the same identifiable characteristics, so that products and/or services can be designed in order to meet the needs of consumers in each segment. When Henry Ford began producing the Model T, he stated: "They can have it in any color they want as long as it black." His basic marketing strategy was undifferentiated with no segmentation.

Today, car manufacturers recognize a myriad of segments, that taken as a whole, constitute the market for cars. There are segments for hot rodders, mothers with children, young families, status seekers, and even states, whereby government air-quality regulations form a segment.

## Forms of Market Segmentation

There are five basic market segmentation forms:

1. Demographic - by age, sex, income.
2. Geographic - by region, urban, or rural.
3. Psychographic - by lifestyle or personality.
4. Benefits - consumer perception: tastes good, feels good.
5. Volume - heavy user, light user.

# Organizational Plan

It is important to spell out in a convincing way your plans for structuring the organization, including a description of the key positions and the people who you have lined up to fill them, with their (hopefully impressive) qualifications. Include an operational plan, describing in detail the type, and, if known, location of facilities that will be required, and equipment that must be obtained. Also discuss what portions of any production work will be done by outside subcontractors, and what parts will actually be done by your people. For the 3 or 4 key people in the company (including each top person in the sales, finance and technical departments), include their resumes at this point, or place them in an Appendix at the end of the business plan, but refer to them here.

# Financial and Technical Data

Here is where you include detailed pro forma financial statements and other important data in support of the conclusions you have set forth in other parts of this business plan. (See chapter 3. *Financial Planning*, for a detailed discussion of these topics). These should include most or all of the following:

## Profit and Loss Projection

This should be on a monthly basis for the first year or two, and quarterly for subsequent years, in most cases.

This projection shows your business financial activity over a period of time (monthly, annually). It is a moving picture showing what has happened in your business and is an excellent tool for assessing your business.

## Pro Forma Balance Sheets

These should show your projected ending financial picture for each of the periods covered by the P & L Statement, (Profit and Loss Statement).

The balance sheet shows the condition of the business as of a fixed date. It is a picture of your firm's financial condition at a particular moment in time, and will show you whether your financial position is strong or weak. It is usually done at the close of an accounting period. It contains the following topics:

• Assets.
• Liabilities.
• Net worth.

## Cash Flow Projection (Budget)

You will need to show monthly or quarterly and cumulative pro forma cash flows, which should tie into the P & L statement and balance sheets for each period covered.

This document projects what your business plan means in terms of dollars. It shows cash inflow and outflow over a period of time and is used for internal planning.

It is of prime interest to a lender and shows how you intend to repay your loan.

Cash flow statements show both how much and when cash must flow in and out of your business.

## Break-even Analysis

In chart form or otherwise, show the level of sales you will need each year in order to break even for that period.

The break-even point is the point at which a company's expenses exactly match the sales or service volume.

It can be expressed in:

1. Total dollars or revenue exactly offset by total expenses or,
2. Total units of production (cost of which exactly equals the income derived by their sales).

## Acquisition Schedule for Fixed Assets

Show an equipment list and loan-dispersal statement about how and when you plan to acquire your equipment. This can usually be appended to the cash flow budget at start-up.

## Other Supporting Data

- Technical drawings of product and/or detailed description of services offered.
- Itemization of capital equipment required and cost.
- Pricing schedule.
- Detailed list of prices for products or services offered, in their different configurations.
- Store layout drawings.
- Floor plans or layout of a proposed manufacturing plant, including a manufacturing flowchart and cost estimates for producing the product, broken down into cost accounting detail.
- Tooling or equipment required for production.
- Description of all tooling that will be required, and the estimated costs.
- Market survey data (primary research).
- Provide any market demographic information that you have developed or obtained.

## Summary and Conclusions

This is where you make your final pitch, so make it convincing. Tell what your total capital requirements are and how much of a safety margin that will provide. Describe who will put up what debt and equity capital to get the business off the ground, and when each infusion of capital will be required. This will tell the prospective investors how much of an owner-ship interest they will be getting for X amount of money.

Reiterate the amount of profits you expect the business to make, when you will make it, and how much of your own money and property you are putting into the venture as evidence of your commitment.

Most outside investors are likely to be leery of investing unless it is clear that you have put your own financial neck on the line, so there's no chance of you simply losing interest and walking away.

## Appendix

This is where you will include an appendix for supporting data. Include whatever you think will be useful to get your point across. You can have more than one appendix.

This chapter has exposed you to the basic elements of a business plan. The next chapter, *Financial Planning*, will detail financial elements that you will need to know before you can draft your own business plan.

# Financial Planning

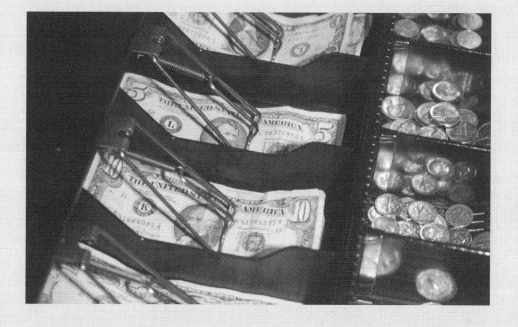

*When someone offers you a lifetime warranty, ask:*
*Whose life, yours or mine?*
*- Dan Titus*

In this chapter we look at financial planning. As a restaurant business owner, you will need to have a basic understanding of the principles presented here. The material presented is from the standpoint of analyzing financial information in order to purchase *any* existing company. This is information you will also use to reinforce your knowledge while you are drafting your business plan. Thanks to Jim Calkins for the use of this material from his book, *Business Buyer's Handbook*.

## Understanding the Health of a Company

The single most important consideration in your review of the company is understanding its financial health. This is done through analyzing and understanding the standard financial measuring tools describing the company. Without knowing how to do this properly, you will invariably ask the wrong questions and get the wrong answers. This, in all probability, will lead to a misunderstanding and possible disaster on your part.

Over the years a standard measurement procedure has evolved for describing the financial health of a company through the use of two health measuring thermometers namely the Income Statement, and the Balance Sheet, or Condition Statement. Both describe the company in very rigid terms representing a fixed time frame.

I present the subjects by going back to the very fundamentals of why you should have financial statements. You may think that you already know how to read a financial statement, but you better be like the major league baseball player who has been playing baseball for fifteen years. Every year he goes to spring training and finds out again and again, that "this is a baseball, and this is a bat, and the fundamental object of the game is to have the bat hit the ball." Most importantly, no matter how long he has played baseball, he learns something new every year. So it is here. You need to go back to the basics and find out what financial statements are and what to do with them. You are bound to learn something you don't already know.

### The Income Statement

To understand income and its effect on the company, you have to start with the very basic reason for the business to exist in the first place: Nothing happens until somebody sells something, albeit a tangible product, or an intangible idea. The meaning here is that you are going to transfer something you have to somebody else in exchange for something. Throughout this chapter, that "something" transferred will be either a physical product or an idea, and that "something" received will be interpreted as cash or cash equivalents, i.e. credit cards, money orders, etc.

The term that was created and employed by accountants universally to define that "something received" is income. My definition as used throughout this chapter is:

Income is the total amount of cash or cash equivalents after payment of applicable expenses received from the transfer of goods or services to a second party.

Throughout this chapter I use the term money as a shorthand description of cash or cash equivalents. Each term, money or cash or cash equivalents is used where the occasion requires.  But, in every case the meaning is identical.

**Critical Basic Point**

In studying the financial health of a company, the number one issue is determining the amount of money the company can generate from sales.  This number, properly derived, defines whether or not the company is a viable entity worthy of your consideration, or one that needs a considerable amount of TLC, including an infusion of new capital to become and remain viable. The structures and analysis provided below will help you understand how to get this information.

Over the years accountants have developed a standard analysis structure that makes it easy to determine the amount of money available to the company to pay income taxes (taxable income), and the amount of money available to the owner for future use (cash flow).

SALES/ REVENUES
*less*
Cost of goods sold or cost of sales
*gives*
GROSS PROFIT
*less*
Selling expenses
*less*
Administrative expenses
*gives*
OPERATIONS INCOME
*plus*
Other income
*less*
Other expense
*gives*
TAXABLE INCOME

..................

*less*
Income taxes paid
*plus*
Extraordinary income
*less*
Extraordinary expense
*gives*
NET INCOME

## 1. Sales (Revenues)

These names are used interchangeably by different accountants in the preparation of financial statements depicting the present operations of the company. While there is no universal usage of each, in general, the term sales implies the transfer of a physical item, e.g., product, furniture, food, clothing, tools, etc. for cash, and revenues indicates the transfer of intellectual property such as advice, or knowledge, e.g., legal or other professional advice for cash.

Therefore, manufacturers, retailers, and distributors tend to use the term sales, while service establishments, such as lawyers, accountants, and consultants tend to use the term revenues.

In both cases, the term represents the total amount of cash or cash equivalents received during a defined time from the transfer of goods or services that relate to the primary activity of the entity providing the goods/services, seller, to an entity receiving the goods/services, buyer. (Usage generally excludes interest received, dividends, and incidental gains/losses from the sale of non-primary items.)

## 2. Cost of Goods Sold  (COGS) - Cost of Sales

These are also used interchangeably by accountants to identify those costs associated with the transformation of some form of raw material into a saleable product. These are further identified as direct costs, indirect costs, and inventory. Note: In manufacturing companies, the transformation takes the shape of changing raw material into finished goods via the process of physically making something. In distributorships, the transformation takes the form of handling, storing, and possibly, repackaging in preparation for sale.  In some instances with distributorships, the original material may be cut, shaped, and/or rearranged before final packaging for sale.  In retail and service companies, the transforming of basic material into a finished product is practically nonexistent.  Therefore, the major item in determining the cost of goods sold for these forms of businesses is that of inventory and the costs  - both direct and indirect - associated with the handling of the inventory.

a) Direct Costs - Applicable to Manufacturers: All the costs directly related to the physical handling of the materials during the transformation production process, including:

• Raw material purchases, including freight.
• Labor directly connected with the handling of the material through production.
• Outside processors performing specific tasks related to the production process.

b) Indirect Costs - Applicable to Manufacturers: All those costs not directly related to the transformation process, but are identified in the support of the processes. They include:

• Supporting labor (maintenance and repair, truck drivers, etc.).
• Subcontract labor (includes all associated costs).
• Utilities for the shop.
• General supplies and tools for the shop.
• Equipment rental.
• Depreciation - (A non-cash expense allocation). Insurance covering the production process and shop employees.
• Other supporting costs that can be legitimately allocated to production processes.

c) Inventory - Applicable to manufacturers and distributors.

Inventory is defined as a cost summation of all of the physical goods connected with the transformation process, including:

• Raw materials not yet used in the transformation process.
• Materials and goods in the process of being transformed into saleable products. Called Work in Process, or WIP.
• Finished products not yet sold.

With distributors the inventory will consist mainly of finished products not yet sold, and, in some instances, WIP where products are further transformed from the original item into different sizes and packages.

As defined above, for accounting purposes, the cost of goods sold is the total of all costs and expenses directly associated with the transformation of raw materials into the saleable products that were sold during a defined period. To determine this:

Start with the value of the inventory (raw materials, WIP charges attached to the transforming product, and fully transformed finished goods ready for sale) remaining unsold at the end of the last accounting period. This is labeled beginning inventory on the current period income statement. To this, you add all of the costs and expenses rightfully charged to the transformation of raw materials into saleable products during the period, both direct and indirect. Next subtract out the total value of everything that remains unsold at the end of the accounting period, labeled ending inventory on the current period income statement. Note: This is done because what you want is the true cost attached only to those units that were sold during the accounting period. Therefore, you subtract the costs of the ending inventory because you have already paid for them, even though the items were not sold, This figure is now ready to serve as the base for the next accounting period with no additional costs attached, i.e., beginning inventory.

For any given period the cost of goods sold is:

Inventory on hand at the beginning of the period (beginning inventory).
*plus*
direct and indirect costs identified with the transformation and handling of the saleable products that were sold during the period.
*less*
cost of unsold materials and saleable products on hand at the end of the period i.e., ending inventory.
*gives*
cost of goods sold during the period under consideration.


## 3. Gross Profit

This is a term developed by accountants to determine how much of the sales/revenues money remains after payment of the costs and expenses directly associated with the transformation/production of the saleable product and truly represents what is available to the company for other operations.  It is determined by:

SALES/REVENUES
*less*
COST OF GOODS SOLD
*gives*
GROSS PROFIT

## 4. Selling Expenses

Costs and expenses that are directly associated with the physical selling of the finished product are selling expenses. They include:

• Sales salaries and commissions.
• Entertainment and other promotions.
• Travel costs of the salespeople and others.
• Advertising, trade shows, and special events.

## 5. Administrative Expenses

Expenses associated with the necessary administrative functions of operating the company are administrative expenses. They include all normal and ordinary office expenses, officers' and staff salaries, bonuses, pensions, non-cash expenses, plus payments made to outside professionals, e.g., attorneys, accountants, consultants.

Normally, interest expense is carried in this category, however some accountants prefer to show it as an other expense (defined below).

At this point, it becomes important to explain what is meant by non-cash expenses, and why they are included in a financial statement.

Non-cash expenses are expenses which are allowed by the IRS as legitimate deductions for tax purposes, but for which there is no cash expenditure.  These include such items as depreciation, amortization, goodwill, and covenant not to compete. A further explanation of each item is given below:

Depreciation is the recovery over a finite time of the purchase/investment costs of a tangible piece of property, (generally termed a capital item), such as a truck, production tool, desk, etc. that has a limited useful life, and is used on a recurring basis by the company in its normal operations. In as much as the company uses these items on a recurring basis in the normal course of conducting its primary business, and as they have a limited useful life which requires the item to be regularly replaced, the IRS allows the recovery of the acquisition costs over a fixed time period through the mechanism of tax savings. The allowed time for cost recovery is rigidly set by the IRS in published tax bulletins. Generally, the allowed recovery time will vary from 3 to 10 years depending upon the particular item, and how it is used.

Because depreciation does not impact the cash needed to support continued operations, (i.e., no cash has been expended) the amount shown on the financial statement is added back to the income as a non-cash item when developing the amount of cash available to the company for future operations.

Amortization is similar to depreciation in being a recovery of allowed costs. However, in this case the item for which the recovery is made is intangible property such as goodwill, covenants given, and/or recovery of the costs associated with a promise given (promissory note), which are not used directly in the primary operations of the company. Although there is no physical wear and tear on the items, they represent an operational cost for which payment was made, or a value was given. Accordingly, they are allowed full cost recovery.

Since there is no wear and tear, the allowed recovery time will vary from a few (5) years to several (30). Similar to depreciation the allowance time is set by the IRS tax bulletins.

Two of the more important items for which amortization is used are a covenant not to compete, and goodwill, which in all probability, you will use if you purchase your company.

A covenant not to compete is a time-limited promise you will get from the owner of the company you purchase whereby he promises not to engage in a similar type of business representing a direct competition to you for a specific period and within a specific geographic area. The time and area will vary greatly depending upon the type of business and its present location. In general, you will be looking for a 5 to 10 year time limit, and 3 to 10 mile geographic limit.

Goodwill is simply a measure of the intangible value of a company developed over its years in business. Basically it is a measurement of how successful the owner has bccn at dcvcloping good customer relations. A value is given because, in a very real sense, goodwill is payment to the owner for doing the hard work of developing a market and strong customer base.

In accounting terms goodwill generally represents the value of that part of the agreed upon price of the company over the book value of the tangible assets held by the company. (See below for definition of book value.) The assigned value is usually shown in the other category of assets on the balance sheet. (See below for explanation of balance sheet.) Since goodwill does have value, the IRS allows it as a deduction similar to covenant not to compete but over a much longer period of time.

The selling and administrative costs and expenses described above are those normally connected with the day-to-day operation of the company, and when deducted from the gross profit will yield what is called operations income.

GROSS PROFIT
*less*
SELLING EXPENSE
*less*
ADMINISTRATIVE EXPENSE
*gives*
OPERATIONS INCOME

As important as operations income is in defining the health of a company, the term does not give the complete picture of how income totally affects the company. To get the complete understanding of the total amount of income available for tax payment and use in future operations, you must account for those income and expense sources that arise from transactions not normally related to the primary income-earning operations of the company, but are necessary to the overall successful operation of the company. These are other income (expense) and extraordinary income (expense).

Other income (expense) items are distinguished from extraordinary income (expense) by being a part of operating the company, but are not directly associated with the primary income earning activities of the company. They are of a recurring nature. In as much as other income (expense) items are a part of the operations of the company they are added to the operations income before determination of income tax. Examples of other income (expenses) are:

• Interest income.
• Recovery of bad debts.
• Gain or loss from the sale of assets, or gains/losses resulting from investments made on behalf of the company.
• Miscellaneous income/expense.

These also can include:

• Fees paid to Board of Directors.
• Investments made on behalf of the company.
• Special purchases or sales made by the company but which are not part of normal operations.

Extraordinary income (expense) are transactions and events that are both unusual in character and infrequent in occurrence. The transactions and events possess a high degree of abnormality, are unrelated or incidental to the ordinary activities of the company, and are of a type that would not reasonably be expected to recur in the foreseeable future. Because extraordinary items are not an ordinary part of company operations and are non-recurring in nature, all applicable income tax relating to the item must be paid separately and apart from income derived from normal operations. Hence, they are added to the income statement after payment of all applicable income taxes due from normal operations, and are added net of taxes associated with the extraordinary item, if any. That is, after payment of income taxes for the specific item. Thus, you are adding after tax items to after tax items.

Examples are gains resulting from money given to the company from a governmental source for relocation or code upgrade, and losses resulting from major casualties such as fires and earthquakes.

Adding other income (expense) to the operations income will yield the amount of income available to the company for future operations before the deduction for income taxes, termed net income before tax or NIBT. All applicable income taxes due from normal company operations are paid from this income. However, to get the total amount of income available to the company for future operations, after payment of income taxes, the after-tax amount associated with extraordinary income (expense) must be added.

## Critical Point

Put a bright Post-it note on this section so you can refer to it quickly. There is no substitute for understanding the financial reporting of a business. The information you gain from Income Statement and Balance Sheet study and analysis lays the foundation upon which all your other investigative data will rest. Financial Reports may seem daunting at first, but don't be put off. Study the reports until you see the story that they are telling. Very soon you will realize the simplicity of their presentation.

For any fixed time period, and from an accounting standpoint, the income available for the company for taxes and future operations is derived by:

Total revenues received during a fixed time period from primary activities
*less*
Cost of goods sold
*gives*
GROSS PROFIT
*less*
Selling expenses and administrative expenses
*gives*
OPERATIONS INCOME
*plus*
Other income
*less*
Other expenses
*gives*
NET INCOME BEFORE TAX
*less*
Income taxes
*plus*
Extraordinary income (after tax)
*less*
Extraordinary expenses (after tax)
*gives*
NET INCOME

The term net income, therefore, represents that portion of the total revenues, after taxes, and extraordinary items, that are available to the company for the future ongoing normal conduct of business.

Understanding the concept of income and how it fits into the operations of the company is fundamental to understanding the financial health of the company. Therefore, it is summarized again below:

As critical as income is to understanding the operations of the company, it does not tell you the number you need most in running your company, namely how much actual cash is available to you from the revenues to successfully operate the company.

### Critical Point
The word income has been generated by accountants as a tool for the purpose of determining the amount of tax you will have to pay on revenues generated from selling your products or services. The term tells you whether you made or lost money from operations, and how much income tax, if any, you must pay.

### Critical Point
Simply put: Cash not income runs companies. Therefore, to determine just how much cash you have after payment of all taxes, you must translate the net income into cash flow.

Fortunately, this process is very simple: Add back those line items that represented a non-cash expense, that is, those line items for which you did not have to write a check, such as: depreciation, amortization, goodwill, and covenants not to compete, etc. that you are allowed (under IRS rules) to deduct as expenses to save taxes.

Accordingly, cash flow is determined by:

NET INCOME
*plus*
Non-cash expenses:
• Depreciation
• Amortization
• Goodwill
• Covenant not to compete
• Other non-cash items detailed in other income/expense and extraordinary income/expense, that can be legitimately added
*gives*
CASH FLOW

Therefore, in evaluating the financial health of a company from an income standpoint, you determine how much cash flow is generated from the sales revenues during any specified time period. Typical examples of cash flow generations from healthy companies will be given following the examination of the other measurable aspect of financial health, namely the condition of the company.

Before presenting those items labeled as representing the condition of a company, it is important to describe exactly what is meant by condition so that as you study the various line items you will better understand why they are there, where they came from, and how they impact the operation of the company.

The word condition of a company closely parallels what you mean in describing the condition of your own body. To be in good physical condition means that you have certain body parts (heart, lungs, kidneys, etc. - assets) that must be present to permit you to survive as a living person. All of these parts must be functioning within specified ranges, that is, not being harmfully degraded by foreign entities (liabilities.) Absent these parts within the specified ranges means that you are not in good condition but, in fact, are sick to some degree.

So it is with an operating company. To be in good financial condition means that the company has all of those parts required to function effectively, and that they are within a specified range. Absent any part within its designated range means the company is sick to some degree.

Those parts that an operating company needs (assets) are:

• Cash.
• Inventory.
• Tools and equipment used to perform the transformation from raw materials to saleable products.
• Physical place to perform the transformation from raw materials to a saleable finished product.
• Means of moving the saleable product to the customer.
• Means of collecting the money from the sale of the product.

Those foreign entities that degrade the vitality of the operating parts (liabilities) are:

• Loans and notes owed to outside entities and/or shareholders.
• Taxes and fees owed to local, state, and federal governments.
• Set asides (accruals) for future payments of loans, taxes, etc.

If the operating parts (assets) are not overly degraded by the foreign entities (liabilities) and can remain within a specified positive range, then the company is said to be in good financial condition.

If, on the other hand, the foreign entities (liabilities) seriously degrade or overtake the operating parts, then the company is sick, or unhealthy to some degree.

For accounting purposes, the names and definitions of the operating parts and foreign entities, and the rules for measuring the degree of the health (condition) of a company have been rigidly defined and applied. These are described below.

## Balance Sheet or Condition Statement

The balance sheet, or as used by some accountants, the statement of condition describes the financial condition of the company at a specific date. It is a time snapshot of the general health of the company related to its ability to stay in business and remain profitable.

The universally accepted term for the health of the company at any given time is net worth or book value.

> **Critical Point**
> In simple terms, the balance sheet, or condition statement displays the sum of everything the company owns - assets - less the sum of everything the company owes - liabilities. If this difference is positive, then the company has a good chance to grow and be successful. If the difference is small, or negative, then the company is in trouble, and may not survive either in the short or long term.

An examination of the respective portions defining net worth is given below:

> **Critical Point**
> As you read through the upcoming paragraphs and the associated definitions of the numbers generated to help you in your analysis, remember that these were developed by accountants as a means of easily defining the operating health of the company. Over the years, these numbers and their method of presentation have been honed and refined to great detail. Therefore, they represent an accurate snapshot of the company's viability. You should become very familiar with the definitions and usage of each factor as they will carry considerable weight in your understanding of the company. Since they are universally accepted and understood by those who operate businesses, I will use names and attendant definitions throughout this book in describing certain points I wish to emphasize.

## Assets

Assets are the tangible and intangible items owned by the company that contribute to its general health. In a human they are the heart, lungs, internal organs, skeleton, and other parts that make up the human body. They are characterized as current assets, fixed assets, and other assets.

Current assets are cash and other acquired resources that are reasonably expected to be consumed or disposed of during a normal operating cycle of the company. They include:

- Cash (On hand in the company, and/or in the bank).
- Receivables.
- Trade sources, less an allowance for bad accounts.
- Non-trade sources.
- Loans receivable from officers and other employees.
- Prepaid payments made on taxes, rent, and loans.
- Inventory.
- Raw materials.
- Work-in-process.
- Finished goods.

Fixed assets are those resources company-owned which are normally not consumed during one operating cycle of the company, are long term in nature, and are active in supporting the operations of the company. Consumption usually takes several years with the costs associated with the resource being recovered for tax purposes through the mechanism of an annual depreciation allowance. (See income statements).

Generally included are:

- Real property (land and buildings) owned by the company.
- Vehicles used in the operation of the company.
- Machinery and equipment used in the operation of the company.
- Tools and dies used in the operation of the company.
- Leasehold improvements on the owned real property that are used in the operation of the company.
- Office furniture and fixtures used in the operation of the company.

Other assets are those resources that normally will not be consumed during the usual operating cycle of the company, and are not active in supporting the operating process. They include:

- Deposits.
- Life insurance, cash value, and goodwill/covenant allocations.
- Investments made on behalf of the company.

The total assets owned by the company are the sum of the three categories:

CURRENT ASSETS
*plus*
FIXED ASSETS
*plus*

OTHER ASSETS
*gives*
TOTAL ASSETS

## Liabilities

Liabilities are the obligations owed by the company that detract from the general health of the company created by the assets. In a human they are the bacteria, fungus, and other disease causing things that detract from the general body health. Liabilities are characterized as current liabilities, long-term liabilities, and other liabilities.

Current liabilities are obligations for which payment will require the use of current assets, will probably be paid within one year from the current date, and include:

- Current accounts payables.
- Trade payable - open accounts and invoices billed to the company from vendors that supply the materials and services used by the company in the normal conduct of its primary business.
- Non-trade payables - Invoices billed to the company from vendors not related to the primary activity of the company.
- Loans and notes payable - The amount to be paid within the current operating cycle of the company. Called current portion.
- Commissions payable.
- Taxes payable.
- Accruals of future payments of deferred items, such as taxes.
- Salaries.
- Pension/profit sharing.

Long-term liabilities are obligations for which all or partial payment will be made in more than 12 months from the current date and require the use of current assets and/or the creation of other obligations. They include:

- Loans and notes payable to a bank or institution, less current portion.
- Loans and notes payable to officers and others.

Other liabilities are obligations for which payment will, generally, be made in more than twelve months from the current date and require the use of current assets and/or the creation of other obligations. Other liabilities differ from long-term liabilities because they include special types of obligations not generally connected with loans and notes, but are more associated with deferred payment of tax and other obligations, penalties due, and purchase of assets not directly connected with the operation of the company. The total liabilities owed by the company are the sum of the following three factors:

CURRENT LIABILITIES
*plus*
LONG-TERM LIABILITIES
*plus*
OTHER LIABILITIES
*gives*
TOTAL LIABILITIES

**Critical Point**
As described earlier, the financial health of the company from the standpoint of the condition is simply the total assets less the total liabilities, or:

TOTAL ASSETS
*LESS*
TOTAL LIABILITIES
*GIVES*
BOOK VALUE (NET WORTH) OF THE COMPANY

The financial health of a company from the standpoint of condition is determined by a critical analysis and review of the assets & liabilities of the company. From accumulated practical experience, accountants have developed an easy way to perform this analysis by using financial ratios. These are a series of numbers that use various parts of the assets and liabilities to describe whether or not the company is in good health and can survive and grow, or in bad health, probably will not survive unless there is an infusion of new cash, and, in many cases, a new management team.

Numerous ratios have been developed to adequately describe the operational health of a company. They are used for various analytical purpoes. However, there are a few key ratios that will give you the basics of what you need to know immediately about the general health of the company under consideration.

Before proceeding with presenting the actual ratios, an explanation of the ratios, their derivation and interpretation is put forth to enable you to have a complete understanding of exactly what the ratio is saying about the health of the company. The names attached to the ratios were developed by accountants and are universal in usage and interpretation. I will first define a series of important ratios and their universally accepted interpretations, then detail the healthy ranges to be used in your analysis.

There are three major categories of operating ratios defining the financial health of the company.  These are:

1. Solvency ratios.
2. Efficiency ratios.
3. Profitability ratios.

## Solvency Ratios

### Current Ratio

Defined as: the total current assets divided by the total current liabilities.

$$\text{total current assets / total current liabilities}$$

Interpreted as: an indication of the company's ability to service its current obligations. Generally, the value is greater than 1.0. The higher the value, the less difficulty the company has to pay its obligations and still maintain assets that will permit continued growth.  A value less than 1.0 indicates the company is over burdened with obligations the company, probably, cannot pay and is in serious risk of not surviving.

### Quick Ratio

Defined as: cash and cash equivalents plus trade receivables divided by total current liabilities.

$$\text{cash and equivalents + trade receivables / total current liabilities}$$

**TIP**
*Key Business Ratios can be obtained from Dun & Bradstreet. Their report,* **Industry Norms & Key Business Ratios***, is a standard reference for industry. Their ratios are developed and derived from their extensive database. Contact them via their Web site: www.dnb.com*

Interpreted as: also known as the acid test, and defines the company's ability to service its current obligations from its most liquid current assets. In this case, a value less than 1.0 implies a dependency on the unscheduled liquidation of inventory or other assets to cover short-term debt.

## Current Liabilities to Net Worth

Defined as: current liabilities divided by net worth (total assets less total liabilities).

$$\text{current liabilities / net worth}$$

Interpreted as: contrasts the funds that creditors have at risk versus those of the owner. A small number indicates a strong company with minimal risk to the creditor's money, implying a high credit rating and ease of obtaining additional debt. Conversely, a high number indicates a greater risk to creditor's money, a lower credit rating, and difficulty in obtaining additional debt.

## Total Liabilities to Net Worth

Defined as: current liabilities + long-term debt + deferred liabilities divided by the net worth.

$$\text{current liabilities + long-term debt + deferred liabilities / net worth}$$

Interpreted as: contrasts with current liabilities to net worth by adding the effect of the long term debt and interest charges on the ability of the company to satisfy creditors. If this number is substantially higher than current liabilities to net worth by approaching 1.0 or greater, then creditors will question the company's ability to continue to service existing debt, let alone additional debt.

## Fixed Assets to Net Worth

Defined as: total fixed assets divided by net worth.

$$\text{fixed assets / net worth}$$

Interpreted as: an indication of the amount of funds the owner has invested in fixed assets.  A high number e.g. greater than 0.75 indicates either, a) the company has low net working capital (assets less liabilities) and, in all probability, utilizes excessive long-term debt to fund the assets, or b) the company is probably not utilizing the assets efficiently and has over-invested itself in fixed assets. In both cases, questions must be raised about the ability of the company to survive in the short term.

## Efficiency Ratios

### Sales to Trade Receivables

Defined as: net sales over a given period divided by trade receivables at the end of the period.

$$net\ sales\ /\ trade\ receivables$$

Interpreted as: measures the number of times the trade receivables turn over in the period included for determining the net sales, normally one year. The higher the turnover, the shorter the time between sale and cash collection.  Allows a direct comparison of the company to industry norms. If the number is higher than industry norms then the company has achieved a relatively strong position in its market. That also indicates the quality of the receivables is better than the norms. If the number is lower than industry norms, then both the trade receivable quality, and the company's market position need to be reviewed to determine continued market viability.

### Day's Receivables

Defined as: the sales/receivables ratio divided into 365 days.

$$365\ days\ /\ Sales\ Receivables\ Ratio$$

Interpreted as: the average number of days it takes to collect the trade receivables. A large number (60 days) means the company may have little control over its receivable collections and be forced to use new debt instruments to maintain production.

## Sales to Net Working Capital

Defined as: net sales over a given period divided by net working capital at the end of the period.

net sales / net working capital

Interpreted as: indicates how efficiently the net working capital (defined as current assets less current liabilities) is utilized in the production of sales. A low number in comparison to industry norms indicates under-utilization of working capital, while an exceptionally high number makes the company vulnerable to hostile takeovers. (Net sales are the total sales less discounts given.)

## Sales to Inventory

Defined as: net sales over a defined period divided by the inventory at the end of the period.

net sales / inventory

Interpreted as: defines how efficiently the inventory is managed. Serves as a guide to how rapidly saleable goods are being moved, and the corresponding effect on cash flow. A low number in comparison to industry norms indicates an unwarranted accumulation of inventory, and a needless expenditure of production funds. An exceptionally high number could signal difficulty in meeting customer demands on a timely schedule by depleting inventory stocks.

## Profitability Ratios

There are three profitability ratios that define the company in terms of its financial health and its value as a candidate for your consideration. These are:

## Return on Sales

Defined as: net income divided by net sales during the accounting period, which is normally one year.

net income / annual net sales

Interpreted as: the fundamental earnings number and indicates the profits earned per dollar of sales. A number above the industry norms indicates a superior company and one that is extremely healthy. A number below industry norms, while not necessarily indicating a sick company, indicates a need for further examination of the causes of the below averages number.

## Return on Assets

Defined as: net income over a given period divided by total assets at the end of the period.

net income / total assets

Interpreted as: the key indicator of the profitability of the company. A high number indicates an efficiently run company, while a small number indicates a poorly run company.

## Return on Equity

Defined as: net income over a given period divided by net worth at the end of period.

net income / net worth

Interpreted as: the ability of the company's owners to realize an adequate return on their invested funds. The higher the number, the more valuable the company is to both the present owners and potential buyers.

All of the foregoing in this chapter have been devoted to giving you the essential factors and their definitions as they relate to the health of a company. At the end of this chapter is a table of norms for the indicated industries. I will also give some key personal observations about what constitutes a healthy company, and which you may find useful in your search and analysis.

The industries focused on are:

• Retail.
• Distributors/wholesale.
• Manufacturing.
• Personal service.

## Critical Point

A note of extreme caution: within each of the general business categories given below, individual companies will vary significantly. A low income, or ratio, for a given company, may indicate a better business opportunity than one one having a high income and ratio. Always remember, as critical as the financial data are, they are not the only parameters that should influence your final buy, or no-buy decision.

Here are a few of my observations regarding the analysis and purchase of companies obtained from my personal experiences. They are offered in no particular order, simply as additional inputs for your consideration.

1. In general, a strong healthy company will show a gross profit of 40 percent or more. While not necessarily a deal killer, a number significantly less than 40 percent needs to be examined closely before final decisions are made. A small gross profit could be as simple as allocating some expense line items that are normally shown in selling or administrative categories as cost of goods sold, or the company could be over charging of direct labor, material purchases, or leased equipment. In either case, a more detailed examination needs to be made to ensure you know exactly why the numbers are the way they are.

2. Always make sure the seller gives you copies of his financial statements willingly and without a long, detailed explanation of why the various line items show the way they do. Also, he should not hesitate in giving you at least the current and last 3-5 years of statements. Extreme Caution: If the owner says "What do you need statements for? Look at what the company has bought me: a new house, a new car, a boat at Newport, a summer estate in Maine, and put all of my kids through college," then he, with a high degree of probability, is taking unreported money from the company, and/or not showing all legitimate expenses on his statements. In which event you'll be in serious trouble if you take over and try to straighten out the books. In this event: run, don't walk,

because you could easily wind up in trouble with the IRS for something you had no control over.

3. While the statements do not need to be audited and certified by an accountant per se, they should be prepared by a certified public account-ant (CPA). This is critical since a good CPA will not risk his license and ability to make a living by knowingly falsifying data for a client.

4. In addition to the internal financial statements, always get copies of the company's income tax returns and compare them with the financial state-ments. The two documents, in all probability, will show slightly different data because of dissimilar requirements of each. However, the income tax return should include a section on reconciling the two documents. If it doesn't, find out why, and determine how significant the lack of the rec-onciliation is. If both documents are prepared by the same CPA, the rec-onciliation will be in the tax return.

5. You should be able to easily determine from the statements exactly how much the seller is taking from the company.

You will find that the vast majority of business owners you talk with are totally honest, and are anxious to put a deal together. They will give you everything you ask for with little difficulty. Nevertheless, you must always be on your guard until you can verify everything.

## Break-even Point

The break-even point is the minimum amount of sales a company must make in order to pay all of its operating expenses, before a profit can be made.

To calculate the break-even point, all that has to be known is what your total overhead is and what your direct costs are as a percentage of sales. The formula is:

fixed costs / 1 - variable costs as a
percentage of sales

## How to Calculate the Break-even Point

For example, Sam's Restaurant is a sole proprietorship that was expected to gross $200,000 last year.

1. Separate and list fixed and variable costs

Fixed Costs (FC) - Are costs that do not vary with the volume of business. These include items like wages, rent, and utilities.

Variable Costs (VC) - Are costs that vary with the volume of sales of the business. Examples include: Food, condiments, and paper products.

### Fixed Costs

| | |
|---|---|
| Labor | $38,000 |
| Payroll tax | 3,800 |
| Insurance | 800 |
| Rent | 9,000 |
| Accounting | 500 |
| Bank service charge | 150 |
| Utilities | 7,000 |
| Telephone | 1,300 |
| Interest | 800 |
| Advertising | 1,000 |
| Depreciation | 1,800 |
| Miscellaneous | 1,200 |
| | |
| Total Fixed Costs | $65,350 |

### Variable Costs

Food & paper products  $77,000

2. Divide total variable costs by total sales:

$$\$77,000 / \$200,000 = 0.39$$

3. Subtract total variable costs as a percentage of sales from one

$$1 - 0.39 = 0.61$$

To determine the annual break-even point, divide the result into the total fixed cost:

$$\$65,350 \, / \, 0.61 = \$107,131$$

5. To find the daily break-even point divide the annual break-even point by the number of days the restaurant is open in a year.

$$\$107,131 \, / \, 256 \text{ days} = \$418.48$$

6. Determine if the store is operating above the break-even point:

a) Annually

Annual gross income - annual break-even point

| | |
|---|---|
| Annual gross income | $200,000 |
| Less annual break-even point | 107,131 |
| Total | $92,869 |

b) Daily

Daily gross income = Annual gross income / total days open

$$\$200,000 \, / \, 256 = \$781.25$$

The conclusion is that Sam's Restaurant is operating well above its break-even point.

## Chapter Notes

# The Business Plan

*You will never "find" time for anything.*
*If you want time, you must make it...*
*- Charles Buxton*

It's sad, but many people are not exposed to the concept of a business plan until going for their MBA (Masters in Business Administration) in college. If I had it my way, students would not be able to graduate high school without at least a basic understanding of the elements of a business plan. In this chapter you will find a sample business plan. Be sure to read Chapter 2, *The Business Plan Primer,* and Chapter 3, *Financials*, so that you will have the necessary footing to draft your own plan using the plan here as an example.

Studies indicate that one of the primary reasons that a start-up business fails is because no business plan was developed, and more importantly, implemented. A business plan is basically a road map so that you know where you are going. Many people, and many consultants, believe that a business plan is nothing more than an equipment list and basic costing information. While these are certainly important, they are only very small pieces of the whole puzzle.

## Business Plan Benefits

Some of the business plan benefits are:

• Provides you with an operating blueprint.
• Assists with the financing of your business. Your banker or investor will insist on seeing your plan.
• Assists with your site development. Leasing brokers will want to see how organized you are.
• Provides a powerful business navigation tool. Defines the business goals and objectives. Allows for plan adjustment - Make your mistakes on paper, it is cheaper!
• Provides a powerful negotiation tool.

If you have ever drafted a business plan, you know that it is a major feat. No one can draft a better plan than you. Sure, there are professionals that can do it for you; however, you are the best person to judge for yourself the current status of your own desires, goals, and financial situation.

There are many stand-alone computer programs on the market that promise a business plan in just hours. While these programs are good at providing general insight into business, they will not provide you with the research necessary to complete a detailed business plan. Can you imagine one of these programs doing a good job if your chosen business happens to be chicken farming in New Zealand? Or, if your chosen business is a wrap store?

You can waste a tremendous amount of time trying to take the easy way out. There is really no simple way. You need to participate in your own future by doing a business plan for yourself or providing the necessary information for a professional consultant to do it. If you do not have the time or resources to do your own plan, be prepared to spend between $2,500 and $3,500 to have the plan prepared.

Depending on the amount of research, this fee can go even higher. The outline used in this plan is simple. We studied several outlines before we basically designed our own. Most business plan outlines are similar. However some are just too detailed and verbose for our liking. Our strategy is KISS i.e., keep it simple stupid (an acronym used by business people).

This sample business plan will provide you with a template to start constructing your own business plan. Take your time and study the table of contents outline; then, thumb through the plan to familiarize yourself with some of the topics.

## Where do I start?

You begin with the business plan financials because the bulk of the plan is written directly from the financial schedules. For example, the Financials Features Section is derived directly from the Pro Forma Income Statements. Pay attention to the assumptions on this schedule - and all of the other financial schedules because they document the thinking behind the numbers. Study the cell formulas of the financial spreadsheets to see how the assumptions tie into the overall statement. You can use the financial statements in this plan as a model or build your own. Remember that the financial portion is the backbone of your plan. Start with financials and then write the rest of your plan.

## This is a Project

You have to look at this as a project. You must break the project down into manageable steps given your most precious current resource: Time. As aforementioned, start with the business plan financials. Once you start, you will find that the sales forecast numbers are the same as the revenue portion of the Pro Forma Income Statement. In other words, when numbers are input into the sales forecast, they are automatically posted to the Income Statement. Next complete the expenses part of the Income Statement i.e., cost of goods sold, operating expenses, and taxes. Then, you will be two thirds of the way done with the financial section.

In the meantime, begin to construct the body of the business plan. Look for a location.  Start your marketing plan. Study your primary competition - the stores in the same business that you are in. Study your secondary competition - the competing restaurants. Plan your menu. Think

**TIP**
*Project manage-
ment task sched-
uling software is
available at the
Web site.*

about your business concept. All of these questions can be answered and plugged into the text body of your plan, while you are working on other parts of the plan.  If you have a number of partners, assign each of them different portions of the plan. Take advantage of the skills of the people in your group; maybe there is an accountant or a marketing specialist. If so, use those skills.

Your business plan is basically an educated guess in many ways. That's the whole idea. You are minimizing risk by creating a plan; that's what pro forma means. It's a forecast, an educated guess.  It's in your best interest to put everything on paper so that any mistakes can be made on paper where they are much easier - and cheaper - to correct.

Enter Murphy.  Murphy's Law states: *"... if anything can go wrong it will."*  Try to anticipate anything that can go wrong in advance. Identify these fail-points.  Don't be afraid to offer one, two, or three back-up plans. For example, you might say "... we have identified a shortfall in revenues in the third quarter in year 2. However, observations have shown that the county fair is in operation for twelve weeks during this same period. We have forecast sales based on the demographics derived from the fair population, and believe that we can post an added gross of $85,000.  This can be obtained by staffing the fair part-time and operating during the daily peak in the evening and on weekends..."

The important thing is to answer all of your questions and above all, answer all the questions to the best of your ability. That way you will have confidence in your plan when you are finished.

## Sample Business Plan

The remaining pages illustrate a sample business plan that you can use as an example to create you own plan. This plan follows the same format presented in Chapter 2, *The Business Plan Primer.*

# Executive Summary

The validity of this business concept, as exemplified in this plan, illustrates a strong potential for success. The plan communicates leadership ability by its operators as evidenced by their business and educational experience. The plan's strong marketing analysis and financial features further identify the operators' business and technical abilities.

The wrap store/smoothie business is poised for long-term growth and is at the beginning of the product life cycle. Therefore, we see a trend in this area for several years. Growth potential is the essence of this plan because it secures a revenue base from which to operate and profit returns for the future.

# The Business Concept

Jim & Judy's Cafe will open with the primary goal of providing convenient, delicious, healthy food as an alternative to fast food. The business will provide nutritionally-conscious consumers with products that complement a busy lifestyle. The products offered will strive to improve the quality of life and, at the same time, familiarize the community with the nutritional "gold mine", which is found only in fruits and vegetables.

While many of us look to the meat and bread food groups to provide the majority of our daily charted nutrients, fruits and vegetables offer many of the same healthy advantages at a lower overall cost to the consumer. Juice has fewer calories and significantly less fat. Because juice requires little digestive breakdown, and is assimilated quickly, consumers get the benefit of energy at a swift rate. We will meet the consumers' need for nutritious foods by providing fresh-squeezed juices.

We will serve fresh-squeezed carrot juice, and fresh vegetable juice, for the powerful nutrition they provide. The nutrients in these fresh raw juices are readily available for absorption and utilization by the body. Carrot juice is naturally sweet and delicious and offers many of the same nutritional attributes. Jim & Judy's Cafe will specialize in a variety of fruit smoothies. Each smoothie will contain juice from concentrate, which is superior in taste to bottled juice. All of the juices are 100 percent natural with no added sugar or preservative. They will be offered as a meal replacement alternative, or as a cool, refreshing treat.

Each smoothie will have two free additional vitamin mix-ins. These will be at the discretion of the customer, and will provide the consumer with nutritional added-value. These mix-ins will include such things as: wheat bran, oat bran, wheat germ, egg protein, soy protein, calcium, ginger, and kelp. The majority of these products come in powder form and blend well with smoothies. We will also offer other nutritional products.

We will serve alternatives to unhealthy snack foods such as traditional salt-laden candy bars and potato chips. An example are energy bars, which are positioned as a low-fat, high-energy snack. These bars are provided in a variety of flavors. Other healthy food substitutes will also be available.

We will serve wraps, which are basically multi-cultural burritos. We have developed a wide variety of wrap menu offerings. *(See a sample menu the at the Web site.)*

Gourmet coffee, selected herbal teas, and a variety of bran and blueberry muffins will round out our menu selection.

## Marketing Approach

We will reach our market segment via retail food distribution by locating in existing shopping and/or power centers. Because the product line is positioned as an alternative food source, the ideal location is a shopping center food court. This type of location is somewhat difficult to find in the cities that we have designated in our primary demographic study.

## Financial Features

Pro Forma financial statements have been prepared for the first 3 years of operation and include: Income Statement, Balance Sheet, Monthly Cash Flow, Cash flow, Revenue Estimates, and Depreciation Schedules. Three-year annual Profit-and-Loss summaries have been prepared, which exemplify revenue growth and marginal increases in the cost of doing business.

Year 1 start-up annual profit after taxes is estimated at $124,255 on total revenues of $436,315. The first two months of operation show a low profit as evidenced on the Pro Forma Income Statement.

A yearly profit-and-loss summary has been prepared. This summary indicates total year 2 revenue, and net profit after taxes at $536,077, and $140,533 respectively. Total revenue for year 3 is estimated at $606,140 and net profit after taxes at $152,626.

### Summary Figures ($)

| Year | 1 | 2 | 3 |
|---|---|---|---|
| Revenue | 436,315 | 536,077 | 606,140 |
| Gross | 294,724 | 347,202 | 429,254 |
| NIAT | 124,255 | 140,533 | 152,626 |

> **NOTE**
> Year 1, 2, and 3 in this example would be sequential years in your business plan. For example, 2012, 2013, and 2014.

All forecasts are predicated on data gathered from statistical studies done from observations and personal interviews with distributors, suppliers, and store owners in the wrap and juice industry.

## Start-up Costs

Total start-up costs are estimated at $91,417 and include a total of $21,360 for leasehold for improvements; however, this figure does not represent any concessions by the lessor, and therefore, is considered to be a worst-case figure. Our strategy is to find an existing facility between 1,000 and 1,150 square feet, which has been a food service facility in the past, and convert it to our needs. The goal is to give it a face-lift, thereby saving some of the costs associated with the start-up. A start-up cost schedule has been prepared and is available for review in this plan.

> *See start-up cost schedule on page 4.31 at the end of this chapter.*

## Current Business Position

Jim & Judy's Cafe is a new start-up venture, which will be operated as a sole proprietorship by Jim and Judy Johnson. The purpose of the business is to provide the consumer with an alternative to fast foods in a cost-effective manner, while at the same time providing the owners with a satisfactory profit. Jim has spent the last six months researching the validity of this concept: *The healthy meal alternative*. This research has included the study of current players in the wrap and juice/smoothie industries. Interviews with suppliers, contractors, and customers have led to the drafting of this business plan.

This plan outlines the validity of this venture by providing a review of the current market.

## Achievements to Date

- Customer profiles have been developed through marketing research.
- Demographic profiles for several cities have been studied.
- A location for the store has been selected: Chino, CA.
- Capital funding has been secured: $80,000 from savings.
- Equipment has been specified and selected.

It must be stressed that Jim and Judy will be putting up the majority of money for this store from their personal savings, thereby giving them a significant equity situation from the start.

## Statement of Objectives

We plan to improve on the existing and successful operations already in the marketplace. All of the competition is marketing the product through retail shopping centers and/or in food courts. Interviews with customers have indicated the need for:

- Noise pollution reduction, which is caused by high-speed blender motors.
- Improved delivery of product during peak demand periods.

We have, to date, investigated several types of blender products and have determined that most of them exhibit offensive whines in the upper mid-range of human hearing. This obtrusive noise can bother customers who are in line waiting to be served. The problem is compounded when delivery of product is slow at peak demand periods. Therefore, the solution to the noise problem is:

- Develop and construct sound traps at the specific frequency of the blender motors. This will be in the form of baffles constructed at the time of build-out.
- Inject pink noise into the environment to mask motor noise.

It should be noted that part of the appeal of a smoothie product is to see it blended in front of the customer. Reducing noise by mixing the product in the back kitchen is not the best solution.

The reason that the blenders in most juice bars make so much noise is because of the high reverberation in these establishments. Recent attempts to deal with this have been to enclose the blenders behind glass or in some cases put the blenders in a plexiglas see-through case in order to reduce the noise. Commercial blenders are also available with noise guards that reduce the noise considerably.

One solution is to enclose the blenders behind a tall sneeze guard that goes from the mixing counter to the ceiling if possible. This provides a wall of glass and acoustically isolates the blenders. However, the blender noise now will reflect off the smooth surface of the glass and bounce off the wall behind it, allowing the sound to get into the rest of the store.

Sound traps and acoustic wall treatments are basically ways to collect or trap reflective sounds. At the location that we have selected, we have a false ceiling, which drops down about four feet. On the backside of this we applied acoustic tiles, which absorb high-frequency sound. These tiles stopped the sound from reflecting off the back wall, therefore, stopping much of it from getting into the rest of the store. Sound traps are more elaborate and, in general, acoustic engineers usually do the designs. They should be incorporated into the design of a new store at the start. Sound traps are basically acoustic cavities that catch reflective sound.

Pink or white noise can be used to mask other sounds. Have you ever heard the noise between stations on the FM dial? That is white noise. Some liken it to a soothing waterfall sound. Many department stores run white noise through their sound systems to make the store quieter. This basically masks clatter sounds in the store and evens out the overall noise level. A fan will exhibit similar characteristics by masking sounds from the outside world.

We have studied the competition regarding the delivery of product, and have found the need for improvement. All of the competitors have only one cash register. Even though they are staffed during peak demand, the bottleneck is the register. Therefore, the solution to the delivery problem is:

- Construct redundant workstations to compensate for higher production needed during peak demand periods.
- Install an additional cash register, which can be opened during peak demand periods.
- Schedule staff to operate workstations and register during peak demand periods.

## Short-term Objectives

- Produce enough revenue to cover costs of operation.
- Create customer awareness of product - see marketing plan.

## Long-term Objectives

- Our goal is to use this store as a model to learn all we can about the operation and this industry. The first year is planned as a proving ground.
- If our concept, financial estimates, and planning are on target, we plan to open more stores with the profits generated by our first store.

# Qualification of Principals

Jim Johnson, who is currently employed by Randolph Construction, has more than 10 years experience as a manager in manufacturing operations as outlined in his resume. Jim holds a bachelor of science degree in business marketing from California State University, San Diego. Jim has been trained in TQMS (Total Quality and Management Techniques) and has implemented/participated in continuous improvement as part of his management philosophy. Jim will manage the cafe and use quality techniques learned throughout his management career.

Judy Johnson, who is currently employed by The Sam Martin Corp., Long Beach, California, has more than 10 years experience in the computer field as a programmer and analyst. She holds an associate degree from Cerritos College, Cerritos, California, and is certified as a data processing programmer analyst.

# Background of Proposed Business

## Product Use

The products sold will be offered for sale in a retail store. The primary products will be wrap sandwiches and fruit smoothies.

# Industry Overview and Trends

In year 1 of this plan, The National Restaurant Association projected the total size of the food-and-restaurant industry in the United States to be $336 billion, and includes the following groups:

**Commercial Food Service:** Full-service restaurants, fast food, commercial cafeterias, social centers, ice cream and frozen yogurt, and bars and taverns. This segment contributes $305 billion to the overall total.

**Institutional Food Service:** Business, educational, governmental, or institutional organizations that have their own foodservice operations. This segment contributes $30 billion to the overall total.

**Military Food Service:** This segment contributes $1 billion to the overall total.

The revenue projections within the commercial segment are as follows:

**Eating & Drinking Places** - $237 billion: includes full-service and limited-service restaurants, commercial cafeterias, social caterers, ice cream, yogurt shops and bars & taverns.

**Food Contractors** - $22 billion: includes industrial plants, office buildings, nursing homes, universities, schools, airline food service, and recreation and sports centers.

**Lodging Places** - $18 billion: includes hotels and motels.

**Other Commercial** - $28 billion: includes mobile caterers, vending, retail host restaurants, and other recreation and sports centers.

Eating & Drinking comprises 78 percent of the total. Food Contractors 7 percent, Lodging Places 6 percent, and Other Commercial 9 percent.

The juice and smoothie market is a sector of the limited-service segment, which includes the fast-food industry. The total size for this industry is $105.7 billion.

# The Product Life Cycle

It is our observation that wrap and juice products are still in between the introductory stage of the product life cycle and the growth stage. New entrants into the industry are pioneering firms. We see the market still developing at this level for the next several years. However, we also see that better-capitalized entrants have aggressive growth strategies and are opening multiple locations. No majors are in the market yet.

The current trend driving the product life cycle is marketing products through strip-mall centers, which are usually anchored by a major food market, or other big-name retailers. Therefore, we are beginning the growth stage of the product life cycle for wraps and juice/smoothies; and, therefore the industry in general, in many metropolitan areas. It can be concluded that the industry has several years to develop within solid growth parameters.

For example, on the West Coast, where the wrap store/juice bar concept has been around for several years, the growth stage is exemplified by some of the following effects and responses:

## Growth Stage

**Competition** - Some emulators.
**Overall Strategy** - Market penetration; persuade mass market to prefer the brand.
**Profits** - High, to take advantage of high prices and consumer demand.
**Retail Prices** - High, to take advantage of heavy consumer demand.
**Advertising Strategy** - Make the mass market aware of brand benefits.

In contrast to the growth stage, we see the introductory stage, which is used as an indicator primarily in the areas where the juice bar concept is new. The following effects and responses evidence the introduction stage:

## Introductory Stage

**Competition** - None of importance.
**Overall Strategy** - Market establishment; Persuade early adopters to try the product.
**Profits** - Negligible, due to high start-up costs.
**Retail Prices** - High, to cover excessive costs of product launch.
**Advertising Strategy** - Aim at needs of early adopters.
**Advertising Emphasis** - High, to educate and generate awareness.

## Strength and Weakness Analysis

### Primary Players

We have used a weighting-scoring model to analyze the competition as well as ourselves.

Basically, the model allows a person to do an objective overview of subjective information. It allows you to weight specific criteria and rank the importance of the criteria; score the criteria, then, total the scores. The score range is 0-5. The final scores are placed on a scale, which is made by multiplying the lowest score and the highest score. Competitors were scored based on observations and assumptions. For example, in the juice/smoothie segment, Samba Juice, the market leader, received more 5s then the competition, including Jim & Judy's Cafe, because they simply have more experience and are better financed than anyone else currently in the market.

*See Chapter 10, Management & Operations for more examples of how to use a weighting-scoring model.*

Our analysis ranks the market players as follows:

| COMPANY | RANKING |
|---|---|
| Samba Juice | 6.1 |
| Jim & Judy's Cafe | 3.9 |
| Juice Too | 3.7 |
| Smoothie Company | 2.9 |

We did not analyze any direct competitors in the wrap segment because there is no competition for our chosen location.

The overall goal here was to see how we stack-up against the competition. We basically tied with Juice Too, which recently opened a new store nearby.

## Company Strengths and Weaknesses

The company's strengths and weaknesses can be identified again, using the weighting-scoring model.

Our weaknesses are as follows:

- Years in Business - zero.
- Short term under-capitalized for growth.
- Retail experience low.

Our strengths are as follows:

- Marketing experience.
- Operations experience.
- Personnel experience.

High confidence is evidenced in core management areas. It is important to utilize these key management skills to gain the retail experience needed to provide revenue growth, which in turn will add to the successful number of years in business.

## Secondary Players

We have secured a location in Town Square. This site is anchored by AMC theaters, Sam's Club, Mervyns, and Target. The restaurant competition within this center is: Marie Calendar's, Expresso Yourself (a small coffeehouse), and Graziano's (a pizza store).

We have prepared an analysis of our secondary competition.

Marie Calendar's came in on top with a total score of 6.25. It is strong in location, resources, and menu offerings, which are very diversified. However, we do not view the company as a threat because its customer base is so different than ours. Marie Calendar's caters to an older clientele and the focus is on sit-down meals. For the most part, no health-conscious meal alternatives are served.

Expresso Yourself is a very small café-style coffeehouse. It serves espresso, specialty coffee drinks, sandwiches, soups and salads. It caters to the early morning crowd, for the most part, by offering specials on coffee and pastries.

We do not see Expresso Yourself as much of a threat because, again, we are offering a healthy-meal alternative as opposed to its menu offerings. We will have to tout the health benefits of coffee in our advertising to help differentiate us in this marketplace.

Graziano's received high scores for resources because it has several locations in the area. It also offers value-pricing. We believe that Graziano's will essentially complement our store because we will get added foot traffic from people who dine there and see our store. We have worked out a trade-out deal whereby we will pass out discount coupons to each other's customers. (See advertising promotion budget).

# Marketing Strategy and Plan

## Market Strategy

*See the section*
*Overview of*
*Market*
*Strategies* in
Chapter 2 *for*
*more details*
*about market*
*strategies.*

Jim & Judy's Cafe will embrace a "nicher strategy" as its marketing strategy. This will allow the company to operate in a market segment, which will avoid clashing with larger competitors. The ideal market niche for the company will display the following characteristics:

- Profitable size.
- Growth potential.
- Neglected by major competitors.
- Can be uniquely served by the market nicher.
- Defensible against majors.

In order to meet these characteristics and still maintain a profitable size, the ideal location for the store would be the Brea/Fullerton, CA., area. This inland area is 35 miles from any competitor. The juice phenomenon started in the beach communities and that is where the major competitors, for the most part, are concentrating their efforts. In the short run, they are neglecting the inland communities. Therefore, these areas fit the nicher strategy that we will be embracing. We will be successful in this market because we will be:

- Locating in new and underserved markets.
- Specializing geographically.
- Focusing on a specific market segment.
- In a unique location.

## Market Segment

Our customer profile is based on research data collected at competitor sites during peak demand month August. The customer profile for our products is the most profitable market segment to address: White females between 15 and 44 years of age. See chart on the next page.

| DEMOGRAPHIC CRITERIA | SEGMENT RANGE |
|---|---|
| **AGE** | 15 to 44 = 80% of Buyers |
| **SEX** | Female to 59%  Male 41 to 48% |
| **RACE** | |
| Asian | 3 to 12% |
| Black | 0 to 1% |
| Hispanic | 6 to 7% |
| Indian | 1 to 6% |
| White | 75 to 89% |

We determined this by surveying customers at three of our competitors sites. We built a weighting-scoring model and profiled customer attendance during all hours of the day, over a one week period.

## The Marketing Mix

We will utilize a marketing mix in order to:

- Define the product.
- Reach specific market segments through the appropriate distribution channel.
- Price product.
- Successfully promote products.

## The Product

We will position our products around our central positioning theme:

*The Complete Healthy Meal Alternative.*

## Product Positioning Model

The four scenarios are as follows and include the elements of price and quality:

| PRODUCT POSITION | PRICE | QUALITY |
|---|---|---|
| Rip-off | High | Low |
| Discount | Low | Low |
| Prestige | High | High |
| High Value | Low | High |

We have determined that prestige and high-value positioning are the best way to address the needs of customers in the target market segment. It must be emphasized that heavily discounting the product in the start-up phase can give the wrong impression to the consumer. Therefore, we have addressed this concern in our promotion strategy. Health is what we are selling. Health has high value.

## Food Products

**Smoothies** - A smoothie is a drink, which is made with fruit or vegetable juice and combined with frozen yogurt, yogurt, or ice cream. Fresh and/or frozen fruits can be added along with the appropriate amounts of ice. These combinations are mixed at high speed in a drink blender to produce a thick frosty fruit/vegetable shake. We like to call them "Yuppie Malts".

**Wrap Sandwiches** – Multi-cultural "burritos" designed as a healthy meal replacement to traditional fast-food.

**Fresh Squeezed Vegetable Juice** - Carrot juice will be offered as well as combination juices made from tomato juice and celery juice to produce a "V8 – style" cocktail.

**Gourmet Coffee** – High-quality coffee will be offered.

**Herb Teas** - A variety of high-quality herb teas will be offered.

**Snackbars** - High-energy snack bars will be offered. The predominant brand will be 'PowerBar'. These will be offered in a variety of flavors: chocolate, vanilla, and peanut butter. This product is positioned as an alternative to unhealthy snacks, such as doughnuts.

**Snack Chips** - A variety of low-sodium/low-calorie chips will be offered. Potato and corn chips will be the core.

**Cookies** – High-fiber/low-sodium cookies will be offered. Core varieties will be: Carob chocolate chip, oatmeal raisin, oatmeal, and peanut butter combinations.

**Muffins** - Bran, banana and blueberry muffins will be offered.

**Salads** - A variety of fresh salads will be offered. These will be point-of-purchase, and in individual serving containers.


## Non-Food Products

**T-shirts** - We will offer T-shirts. They will bolster brand recognition and help foster customers loyalty. They will picture the store logo.

**Caps** - We will offer caps. They will be worn by all store personnel and will be available to customers for purchase.

**Coffee Mugs/Sports Container** - We will offer coffee mugs and sports containers. These products will have logos, which will bolster product and brand recognition.

## The Place

### Distribution

We will reach the target market through retail distribution of the product. The facility requires between 500 and 700 feet of operating space; however, location selection has concentrated on sites that are between 1,000 to 1,200 square feet because these bay sizes are more standard and therefore more readily available.

### Location

We will concentrate our efforts on consumers in five mile radius of the store. The criteria for the site selection of the store is:

- Location of the store in reference to the owners' home.
- Demographic profile of the customer.
- Demographic profile of cities in which the current concept is now being carried out.

*See the Web site for details on how to conduct a customer demographic profile.*

Consideration has been given to business traffic, store location to residential communities, and major educational institutions.

Based on this information, the Brea/Fullerton area most closely mirrored the demographics of competitors now in business. Samba Juice, who is the current leader, is located in Santa Ana, CA., between John Wayne Airport and California University at Irvine. This provides them with good diverse customer base.

## Pricing Strategy

> *"...In the store we make wraps and smoothies...In image*
> *we sell HEALTH..."*

Interviewing industry sources and comparing competitors' price lists, which appear on their menu selections, we developed the pricing schedule. The basic formula applied here is: Retail price = 4 X COGS, (Cost of Goods Sold).

We used competitor prices for the development of our sales forecast, and the preceding formula on items not available for comparison on these menus. The pricing goal is to offer a product line that addresses each customer's perception of value. We will market different products for different perceived value, thereby hitting every potential customer's "hot button". This goal will be accomplished while staying within the limits of our product-positioning stance.

Examples:

- **Super Smoothie** - A full day's worth of vitamins in every sip.
- **All-N-One** - Berrything except the kitchen sink.

Since our store will be located in Ontario, which has a large Latin population, we have decided to institute an *odd* pricing scheme, which will address the perception of value to this and other demographic segments. For example, we have decided to price some of our smoothies at $2.99 rather than at $3.00 in order to reinforce price value to some customers. In contrast, we have decided to price some smoothies at a high price, knowing that there are certain individuals (innovators) who only buy the best of everything.

## Discounts

We will offer discounts on our smoothie products on a continuing basis. This discount will be in the form of a punch card, which will provide the customer with a free smoothie product after nine smoothies have been purchased.

Other promotions designed to educate the customer about the product and the company will be introduced. These promotions will be in the form of percentage discounts or two-for-one specials.

## Promotion Strategy

### Parameters

- The promotion budget will be distinctly limited.

- The marketing philosophy reflected in this plan emphasizes market segmentation and sharply defined target markets, which are available from our customer profile demographics. Scarce marketing promotion resources will only be invested in high-return segments.

- This plan focus is on the introductory phases of initial opening and secures a budget for continued promotion within these segments.

During the start-up/pioneering stage of the business, the goal will be to build the store's identity. This will concentrate around the store opening, and initial product rollout. The objectives will be:

- Build awareness of our store.
- Present and enhance image of our store.
- Point out a need and create a desire for the product.

The promotion will explain what the store is, what products the store has to offer, why it is in business, where it is located, when people can obtain products, and how people can reach the business.

We will be using pull strategy in order to get customers into the store. Advertising will be the primary vehicle used to accomplish this goal.

## Media Planning

To date, local advertisers have been contacted and are assisting with marketing demographics for different locations. We have established an initial rollout budget of $2,000 with a monthly ad budget of $600 to spread across different media:

- Local penny saver.
- Local newspaper - schools.
- Flyers/coupons.
- Co-op advertising.
- Promotional events.

## Promotional Budget and Creative Planning

Ad design will be targeted at each demographic segment. Most advertisers will create an ad as part of their overall package. A sketch and logo artwork will be supplied for their use in designing and distributing the ad.

The following chart outlines our advertising/promotion budget.

## Media Promotional Budget ($)

| MEDIA | 1 X Cost | Week | Month | Mo. Cost |
|---|---|---|---|---|
| Campus news | | | 75 | 75 |
| Flyers | | 12.5 | | 50 |
| Coupons | | 15 | | 60 |
| Stand-ups | 250 | | | |
| Banners | 850 | | | |
| Newspapers | | | 320 | 320 |
| Co-op ads | | | 50 | 50 |
| Publicity | 0 | 0 | 0 | 0 |
| News | | | 25 | 25 |
| **Total Costs** | **$1,100** | **$27.5** | **$470** | **$580** |

We have budgeted $2,000 for our grand opening; $1,000 will be used for small giveaways, promotions, and special events. The rest will be used as follows:

Total one-time start-up ad costs are $1,100. These costs are spread across promotional events, stand-ups and banners. Stand-ups are part of our initial rollout budget of $2,000.

Stand-ups are 8x11-inch laminations that have a cardboard photo stand glued to the back so that they function as a displays. We will put these in local business's break rooms and staff coffee rooms with a stack of flyers and/or coupons in front. Many businesses will even let us put these displays right next to their cash registers. This will advertise our products and entice customers to the store via the coupons offered. We have budgeted for 25 stand-ups at a cost of $10 each.

Banners will be used to reinforce our image throughout selected businesses in the area. These are part of our rollout budget of $2,000. We will negotiate with businesses in the area to host a smoothie day periodically in exchange for product discounts for the employees. We will hang a banner in their facility for at least one week prior to the event. This procedure will also be used at schools in the area. Banners will also be draped on a wall at special events on weekends. We have budgeted for 10, 3x8-foot banners at a total cost of $850.

We will utilize flyers and coupons on an ongoing basis. We have budgeted for 250 flyers to be distributed weekly. Flyers cost $50 for 1,000; we will spend $50 per month.

Co-op ads are exchanges and trade-outs with local merchants. We will distribute their coupons if they distribute ours. We will also cooperate with in-group advertising efforts whereby we will share ad space with other local businesses that complement our products. We have budgeted $50 per month for co-op advertising.

We have budgeted $75 per month for ad space in the local college and high school newspapers.

Newspaper ads basically mean that we will spend $320 across local news magazines and/or flyer magazines and typical daily newspapers: West Coast Media, The Coupon Advantage, The Pennysaver, and The Champion Newspaper. We will rotate zones on a periodic basis to get ad exposure in different areas.

Publicity is basically *free* advertising. We will provide articles on health-related issues and juicing to our customers, and news media for publication in their newsletters and/or newspapers. Because publicity has an estimated value – in this case $100 per month – it is a direct savings to the advertising promotion budget.

Creative planning and production costs are included in the budget. Judy Johnson, who is proficient at art, will develop all artwork for the flyers and coupons via computer.

Ad design will be targeted to each audience. Most advertisers will create an ad as part of their overall package.

## Market Penetration

Revenue forecasts for the year one through year three are shown in the chart below. We estimate the local juice bar market for our area to be $1.5 million annually. We have included our primary competition in the area: Juice Too, and Smoothie Company. We have included estimates for all other stores selling like products, which is equal to $100,000 yearly.

## Summary Figures ($)

| Year | 1 | 2 | 3 |
|------|------|------|------|
| Revenue | 436,315 | 536,077 | 606,140 |
| Gross | 294,724 | 347,202 | 429,254 |
| NIAT | $124,255 | $140,533 | $152,626 |

## Potential Market Share (%)

| POTENTIAL MARKET SHARE | Year 1 | Year 2 | Year 3 |
|------|------|------|------|
| Jim & Judy's Cafe | 21 | 25 | 36 |
| Juice Too | 36 | 34 | 29 |
| Smoothie Company | 36 | 35 | 30 |
| Other | 7 | 6 | 5 |

The preceding charts indicate approximately a 15 percent rise in our market share over the next few years. This assumes that all other parameters stay the same in the area. Also, we expect to do better in the immediate area because Smoothie Company is some distance from our store. We anticipate, once the customer base is educated, to win share away from the 7 percent, other competitors in the area. These are coffeehouses and restaurants that offer sandwiches and smoothies on their menus but do not specialize in them.

# Organizational Plan

## Owner/Manager

Jim Johnson, who is currently employed be Randolph Construction, has more than 10 years experience as a manager in manufacturing operations as exemplified in his resume. Jim holds a bachelor of science degree in business marketing from California State University, San Diego. Jim has been trained in TQMS techniques and has implemented and participated continuous improvement as a management philosophy. Jim will manage the store and employ quality techniques learned through Jim's management career.

Jim says, "The goal is to satisfy customer needs and wants by working as a cohesive team. This includes empowering employees to solve problems, and allowing suppliers to be in on key business decisions."

Jim is familiar with retail food management and has experience in the industry. In high school, he worked as a clerk and later as an assistant manager in the fast-food industry.

Judy Johnson, who is currently employed by The Sam Martin Corp., has more than 10 years experience in the computer field as a programmer and analyst. She holds an associate degree from Cerritos College and is certified as a data processing programmer analyst.

## Consultant

CBM Payroll Services:

CBM Payroll Systems will consult with us regarding financial issues and will keep the books for the operation.

## Service Counter Personnel

Service Counter Personnel are basically the employees who will work in the store. They will serve the customers, work the register and do all the necessary tasks to work the store.

## Manuals & Procedures

We are in the process of writing a personnel manual, which will establish policy and general guidelines for all employees.

We are in the process of writing an operations manual in order to establish basic procedures. This manual will serve as a training tool and serve as a continual reference.

## Capital Equipment Budget

We estimate that equipment will cost $56,257. This figure includes production equipment, signage, tables, office, and other equipment.

## Leasehold Improvements

This is for the 1,500-square-foot location. This facility is basically a remodel, <u>and already has major restaurant fixtures in place</u>.

**LEASEHOLD IMPROVEMENT SCHEDULE**

| Item | Cost |
| --- | --- |
| Floor installation | $3,300 |
| Cabinets and tables | 8,500 |
| Paint | 1,300 |
| Custom 2" window blinds | 850 |
| Custom stainless steel counter tops | 1,500 |
| Water heater | 500 |
| Custom stainless steel dish sink | 750 |
| Remodel for employee changing room | 600 |
| Bathroom fixtures | 250 |
| Electrical work | 1775 |
| Plumbing work | 485 |
| Wall repair | 650 |
| Recondition floor | 500 |
| Misc. fixtures | 400 |
| **TOTAL** | **$21,360** |

## Store Decoration and Layout

In order to maintain the flavor of the shopping center, which is done in a Spanish style architecture, we will basically "pull" into the store as much of this feeling as possible. The store will be a cross between Southwest and Spanish styles. This will work well with our goal to have the store appeal to some of the demographics for the area - Latin - and at the same time provide an inviting environment, which will address our primary target customer profile.

In order to save money, we will go to the city and get copies of the plans that are on file for the previous business at this location. This will allow us to do a basic mark-up for plan submittal for the construction and health department permits. We will act as our own general contractor, doing some of the work ourselves and hiring contractors to do the painting, plumbing, electrical, cabinet work, and floor installation.

In the customer area, we will replace the carpet with Mexican style 12-inch floor tiles. The service area will have new 6-inch restaurant quarry tile installed. We will retain the vinyl flooring in the food prep area, kitchen area, and the bathrooms.

We have designed a custom stainless steel counter top that will hold the juice extracting and juice dispensing equipment. The unique thing about the design is that it allows for quick clean up and removal of vegetable pulp.

The vegetable juice extractor and citrus juice extractors sit on the counter; below each is a custom stainless steel drawer with a conventional kitchen trash container inside. Holes will be cut into the counter top so that pulp can be discarded directly from the machines into the containers. We will line the inside of the trash cans with plastic garbage bags. When it comes time to empty the cans, it will be just a matter of sliding out the drawer, and removing the bag.

All service countertops and tables in the store will be made with a slate-colored laminate. The color is marbled gray-orange-pink. This beautiful finish will resist juice stains. Side panels for the service cabinets will be dove gray and feature the slate color framed in solid oak.

We will also have two large bar tables at the north end of the store with seating for eight.

All chairs, custom furniture and pictures will be light wood in order to enhance and emphasize the natural aspects of the store.

The paint will be French-white, which has a tinge of rose. Painting will be done by a contractor before the floor is installed.

The menu boards will be on the north wall because the roof over the service area is too low to allow posting a menu in typical fashion over the back of the area. This works out well because it will give the customers a place to mingle and look at pictures and descriptions of offerings.

All artwork in the store will be proprietary in order to reinforce the products in the store.

## Suppliers

To date, all menu items have been sourced. Costs and pricing have been calculated for wraps, juice, hot beverages, and smoothies. These items are on the menu draft.

## Financial Projections

### Overview

Projections have been prepared as evidenced by the following schedules. We have prepared a complete set of financials for year 1, year 2 and year 3:

- Sales Forecast.

- Pro Forma Income Statement.

- Pro Forma Balance Sheet.

- Cash Flow Statements.

*See the Web site for details about how to use restaurant financial spread-sheet templates.*

We have $80,000 from savings to invest in this venture, and we have secured a loan of $20,000. This amount is enough to cover all start-up costs. We have the potential to call in an additional $20,000 for working capital when we receive repayment for a loan.

Income statements serve as operating statements. These give an overview of all revenue and expenses. They also serve as a labor budget and total operating budget for this start-up venture.

We anticipate low revenues for the first few months of operation. Jim will not take a salary until the first month of the third year. Income statement figures can be summarized in the following chart:

## Pro Forma Income Statement Summary

| YEAR | REV | COGS | GROSS | NIBT | NIAT |
|------|-----|------|-------|------|------|
| 1 | 436315 | 414591 | 294724 | 165673 | 124255 |
| 2 | 536077 | 188875 | 347202 | 187377 | 140533 |
| 3 | 606140 | 176886 | 429254 | 203502 | 152626 |
| Totals | $1,578,532 | $507,352 | $1,071,180 | $556,552 | $417,414 |

We have included marginal cost increases for utilities and COGS for the first and second year of operation. Also, labor will fluctuate during peak months for the second half of these years. We will add additional labor starting in June through the end of the year to cover demand and the added service required for the holiday season.

NIAT figure accrues on the Pro Forma Balance Sheet in the cash line item. If possible, we expect to pay off the capital loan of $20,000, in year 2; however, the financial statements currently reflect a loan payment schedule for this amount.

We will build a substantial equity position of $204,228 at the end of the first year. This figure jumps to $344,276, by the end of the second year, and to $476,902 at the end of the third year. This is here primarily for illustration. If we pay off our loan and/or invest in other store ventures, this figure will change.

Our figures represent a positive outlook for our operation. We believe that this will put us in a good position to invest accumulated profits and equity into other store(s).

## START-UP COST SCHEDULE

| | |
|---|---:|
| Rent: Security deposit and 1st month | 3,500 |
| Leasehold improvements and fixtures | 21,360 |
| Equipment | 56,257 |
| Licenses and tax deposits | 750 |
| Phone and utility deposits | 1,500 |
| Professional services: Accounting/Legal | 750 |
| Start-up inventory | 3,000 |
| Insurance | 1,600 |
| Grand opening & advertising | 2,000 |
| Miscellaneous | 700 |
| **TOTAL COSTS** | **$91,417** |

# Summary and Conclusions

The wrap and juice business is poised for long-term growth and is at the beginning of the product life cycle. We see a solid growth trend in this area for many years. This growth potential is the essence of this plan because it secures a revenue base from which to operate and profit returns for the future.

The owners will commit $80,000 and an additional $20,000 in secured loans to the fruition of this venture. The strong equity position of this endeavor secures a solid base for operations and provides a sound financial foundation for the future.

The validity of this business concept as exemplified in this plan illustrates a strong potential for success. The plan communicates leadership ability by its operators as evidenced by their business and educational experience. The plan's strong marketing analysis and financial features further identify the operators' business and technical abilities.

## Chapter Notes

# Site Selection

*To improve the golden moment of opportunity, and the good*
*that is within our reach, is the great art of life.*
*- Samuel Johnson*

This chapter is designed to educate you about the different locations for your store. Whether a shopping center or a shopping mall, it will explain what you need to know in order to select the location that is best for your business.

# Site Selection Basics

There are no rule-of-thumb theories when it comes to selecting a site for a restaurant. Some retail businesses use sophisticated high-tech techniques and others use simple low-tech observation. For example, 7-Eleven store locations are determined using an elaborate quantitative mathematical model; In-N-Out Burger restaurant locations, a popular West Coast burger chain, are chosen by flying over prospective sites and surveying the traffic flow patterns.

Location is the most critical part of your entire planning process. For a wrap store, or any retail venture for that matter, foot traffic is the most critical criteria. Foot traffic should be good for all hours of operation. Do not dismiss a location because the rent is expensive. If foot traffic is good, you will want to be there as opposed to a location that has lower rent and poor traffic.

Here are some basic guidelines to assist you in site selection:

- Identify traffic patterns.
- Identify types of locations.
- Maintain a solid business concept.
- Develop a customer profile.
- Locate near business and population centers.
- Interview business owners and suppliers.
- Have good store visibility and accessibility.
- Research zoning requirements.
- Trust your instincts.

## Identify Traffic Patterns

There are two kinds of traffic patterns that can develop for a retail operation. It is important to be aware of these patterns because you will select and market your location differently for each. The two patterns are:

- Transient traffic patterns.
- Closed-loop traffic patterns.

### Transient Traffic Patterns

Transient traffic patterns are those found where large numbers of people typically gather - in airports, tourist attractions, sports arenas, amusement parks, regional malls, and performing arts centers. People come from a wide area and are not repeat customers on a day-to-day basis.

### Closed-loop Traffic Patterns

Closed-loop traffic patterns are those found in densely populated areas - large office buildings, business and industrial parks, hospitals and medical centers, collage and university campuses, and military bases. Customers in this category will generally come back to your restaurant and generate repeat business for increased sales.

## Identify Types of Locations

There are several types of retail locations. Following are some definitions and details about some of the most popular restaurant locations.

### Regional Malls

Regional malls are large shopping centers containing a mix of different types of businesses. For the most part, malls are enclosed; however, in recent years the popularity of the outside mall concept has begun to reappear in areas where the winters are mild, as evidenced by The Block, in Orange, CA., and Down Town Disney, in Anaheim, CA. Accessibility to malls is usually from major thoroughfares, which allow them to service vast markets.

Malls are great for traffic counts; the better ones can attract a large number of potential customers. However, all that traffic can cost you. The rent at major malls is usually higher. The CAM (an acronym that stands for Common Area Maintenance) charges are higher and you might be required to participate in cooperative advertising.

### Shopping Areas

Shopping areas serve the community, thereby directly benefiting from the existing population. For example, a downtown area in a city benefits from local office workers or residents. In some cities, these shopping areas also draw residents who live in nearby suburbs because they may offer a positive entertainment or shopping value.

Shopping areas can be expensive retail areas and may lack sufficient parking for customers. Most of the traffic in shopping areas comes from office workers. Business traffic generally is limited to lunchtime and dinnertime hours. Therefore, weekends may not be as busy as at other locations, unless there are other draws or residents in the area.

### Neighborhood Shopping Centers

Neighborhood shopping centers are usually anchored by supermarkets, major drugstores, or other large retailers. They may also benefit from smaller diversified merchants in the center such as, cleaners, beauty salons, flower shops, and small restaurants, etc. These locations derive their traffic from the local community, and are preferred by most retailers and restaurateurs. Larger regional centers and malls may have restrictions; however, most neighborhood shopping centers have fewer restrictions, which can make them more attractive for a start-up venture.

### Strip Centers

Strip centers are smaller versions of neighborhood centers and are not generally anchored by a large grocer or drugstore. Typically, the newer strip centers are anchored by a food court, which may have major quick-service retail operators on site, such as Starbucks Coffee, Baskin-Robbins, and Sub-way.

## Maintain a Solid Business Concept

Paramount to any site selection process is the ability to clearly identify your business concept. This can be stated in defining what kind of restaurant you are. Your site selection will be different for a fine-dining seafood restaurant than it would be for a quick-service, Italian food take-out restaurant. You might consider a beach or waterfront location for the former in order to set the ambience for the restaurant. However, a quick-service (fast-food) operation might lend itself to any variety of locations, thereby being more flexible when it comes to picking a site.

A wrap and smoothie concept is generally a quick-service restaurant, where customers come to get their food, then leave. Seating is usually very limited; the emphasis is on getting the customers their food quickly, so that they can be on their way.

## Develop a Customer Profile

A customer profile should include demographic characteristics, such as: race, age, income, sex, and buying preferences. An easy way to obtain this information is to survey your potential customer population. You can do this by looking at existing customers of competitors in your area. The assumption being that this population base will mirror your customers' characteristics.

Once you have a customer profile, find a site that matches it by researching city demographic data. This data is available at city offices and leasing brokers. Another great source for this information is the Internet. The U.S. Census Bureau has demographic data for all cities in the United States (www.census.gov).

## Locate Near Business and Population Centers

Locate your restaurant near other businesses that will help drive people to your location. A food court is an excellent location if there are repeat customers who work or shop in the area. Even though you will have competitors in this kind of location, they are really indirect competitors because restaurants in a food court complement one another.

Locate your business near other businesses like grocery stores, drugstores and gyms. Your neighbors can help your visibility - particularly if they have good traffic.

Office buildings and colleges are population centers that can add traffic to a location. When surveying a location, be sure to canvass the area within a five-mile radius to determine the extent or concentration of these population centers. Confirm their existence.

## Visibility and Accessibility

Your customers will need to be able to see you and access your restaurant. Good visibility from your traffic points is a must. If you locate in a shopping center, your sign should be visible from the street. If you locate in a mall, people walking about need to see your sign and store frontage.

Look for potential problems in accessibility to your store. There might be a parking lot configuration that hinders customers from walking to your store: Once they have parked their vehicles, they have to cross a busy driveway entrance to the shopping center. There might be a bank of handicapped parking in front of your store, or a bank of 10-minute parking zones that could hamper accessibility.

Above all, look for obstacles. Look for one-way streets, solid meridians that can prevent customers from entering a location. Look for easy traffic flow. Make sure pedestrian traffic has easy access to your store.

## Interview Business Owners and Suppliers

Once you have chosen a potential location that meets the demographic requirements of your customers' profile, it is important to interview local business owners and suppliers. Simply go into the stores in the area and ask them how business is. Ask them to compare their current business situation with that of a year or two years ago. You can learn a tremendous amount about what is happening in an area by talking to existing businesses.

Interview suppliers as they are making deliveries. Delivery drivers have a keen sense of what is going on. Ask them how the volume of supplies has been for a given period. For example, you could ask about the volume of supplies that has been delivered over the past several months for a local restaurant. This can give you an idea of the high and low spots in revenue over that time period.

## Research Zoning Requirements

The old adage "It is better to be safe than sorry" applies when it comes to zoning restrictions. You need to check out what is permitted in regard to maximum area that can be built on a site. Be sure to find out about signage and or parking restrictions that apply in the area. Your leasing agent and landlord will have details about these and other zoning restrictions. Another good source for zoning requirements or restrictions is construction contractors. To be safe, check with the appropriate government zoning agency in any city you are considering as a location.

## Trust Your Instincts

Your instinct is a critical factor in the site-selection process. It can be a valuable tool. Do not fall into the trap of confusing emotions with instinct. Your emotions can get you in trouble because you may be apt to ignore vital aspects of the site-selection process in order to appease them. For example, you might get excited about a previous restaurant location because it has all the infrastructure for a restaurant: Sinks, cabinets, and cooking hoods. You might sign a lease only to find that there is no foot traffic at the location. Conversely, you might find a site that just feels good. The site may be located in a food court, and have all the elements you are looking for, such as: outside patio, plenty of foot traffic, and great ambience.

## Chapter Notes

# Leases & Negotiation

This chapter will introduce you to the main elements of commercial real estate leases, and what to look out for. It details percentage rent deals, per-square-foot rent, and many of the rent provisions, such as CAM, that you will be responsible for. Finally, you will be exposed to some basic negotiating strategy.

# Leases

Leases can make or break your business. Signing on the dotted line without taking the necessary steps to understand them can be lethal to a business.

Landlords, by the very nature of their business, have an unfair advantage when it comes to leases. They write them. It is up to you and your advisory team to decipher the language.

You will be competing against the major chains for store space. Landlords prefer to lease to established chain restaurants. These big fish typically bring to the table more resources; hence, more revenue. Leasing agents are quick to see dollar signs for high commissions and percentage rent deals - the leasing agent/broker is the contact person you will be dealing with when you negotiate your lease. They are usually paid a commission for their efforts.

The economy, supply, and demand have a lot to do with the landlord's negotiating position. If there is only minimal space in the shopping center you are looking at, there will be a tight demand for space; hence, your negotiating position will be diluted. If the economy is slow and there is a lot of space available, your position will be better. Beware that if demand is tight for space and you are looking for space below 1,500 square feet, you will be considered a small fish by the leasing agent, and for the most part the agent will be hesitant to negotiate with you.

## The Rent is Due

Rent is the stated payment at fixed intervals for the use of a house, commercial structure, or land.

Landlords exist to collect rent. Period. This is why they are in business. They expect the terms of the lease to be honored. That means payment on time, according to the terms of the contract. If you skip a rent payment, expect to pay penalties. If you default on the lease by moving out of the space, expect to be sued for the remaining lease payments due on the lease, taxes and CAM charges, plus any sales commissions due to the broker who sold the lease, plus court costs. If you default on rent payments, the landlord's goal will be to get you out as soon as possible, and rent the space to another tenant. The landlord's goal will not be saving your business.

Therefore, I encourage you to start looking for a consultant. Real estate brokers have extensive knowledge with contracts and charge less for their services than lawyers. Never sign a lease until you have had an experienced person, at the bare minimum, review it. Find a lawyer that is familiar with restaurants because other lawyers will not have the necessary specialized experience. Consultants' fees will be worth every cent! Never sign a lease until you understand every aspect of the lease contract.

## Percentage Rent Deals

Landlords usually charge established chain restaurants percentage rent, which is rent based on a percentage of gross sales. They do this because they know that the chains make more revenue than mom-and-pop operations. Therefore, they can maximize rent revenues. As a new start-up, you should avoid these types of deals. In reality, they won't offer the new restaurant start-up a percentage deal because they know that you will probably make less than a major chain store. If you gross less; they make less rent.

If you do find yourself, getting involved with this type of deal, be sure to define word-for-word in the lease contract what gross sales are. Exclude as much as you can from gross sales. After all, you will be paying rent based on the total figure. Landlords will more than likely put a clause into the lease contract that will give them the right to audit your books. This is how they will know how much rent to charge you. If this is the case, insist that the percentage rent not start until you have met your break-even point.

Many major and anchor tenants have a percentage rent clause in their leases. However, they are good at negotiating - they are big fish. For example, the total impact of a clause can be lessened by adjusting the language in the lease. Adjustments to gross income can be made by deleting certain items they sell and taxes from gross income. They can recapture their costs for triple net expenditures. They can create an artificial *break point*, which is the sales level at which they start paying percentage rent.

Many industry consultants do not feel that landlords who charge market rents, have provisions for rent escalation clauses, and are reimbursed on all or most of their costs, should have the ability to participate in a tenants increased sales level. Percentage rent clauses are normally long and drawn out in legal language. Here is an example:

Assume you have a small restaurant that has approximately 1,500 square feet and your rent is $25 per square foot per year, triple net. (Triple net is another term for CAM, taxes and insurance, which is explained later.) Simply stated, your minimum annual rent is $37,500. Let's also assume that you have a five percent (5%) rent clause. This means, your break point (once you reach a specific gross sales level, you start paying additional rent to the landlord) is $750,000 ($37,500 divided by .05 = $750,000). If you reach a total gross sales of $1 million for the year, your additional rent from the percentage rent clause will be $12,500 (5% of all gross dollars over $750,000 or in this assumption $250,000), which means your true rent for the year is $33 per square foot, not the agreed to $25 per square foot. (Base rent plus additional percentage rent of $12,500 = $50,000 total annual rent. $50,000 annual rent divided by 1,500 total square feet = $33 per square foot.

Many industry experts state that when negotiating a percentage rent, minimum rent, or escalation clause, landlords may attempt to find out what you expect to net or gross from your prospective store by asking you for your projections of sales at their site. Do not tell them as they can use that information against you in negotiations.

## Per-Square-Foot Rent

Rent that is paid based on the size of your store is called per-square-foot rent. Basically, you are charged rent based on the foot print size of your store. For example, if your store is 2,000 square feet and the rent is $2.00 per foot, per month, your rent will be $4,000 per month.

Landlords will define the type of square footage in the rental contract. Be aware what they are talking about. Are they talking about total net rentable square feet, gross floor area, net usable square feet or some other measures.

## Rent Provisions

Paying rent seems like a straightforward deal: Give the landlord the rent at the end of the month, then go on with your life. While this may be true for residential leases, it is not the case for commercial leases. You must educate yourself about major commercial provisions. Provisions are clauses in legal documents stipulating some specific thing.

We have discussed a couple rent provisions already: Percentage rent and per-square-foot rent. Now let's take a look at some other rent provisions.

## Term of Lease

Restaurants generally require more start-up costs in the way of lease-hold improvements - also, known as tenant improvements, or TIs for short. Moreover, restaurants incur higher specialized plumbing, lighting, and fixture costs than other businesses. They also must comply with government safety regulations. For example, restaurants must provide ADA - *Americans with Disabilities Act* - compliant restrooms.
Therefore, in order to fully amortize these costs and provide an adequate return on investment, restaurants usually want to have longer length-of-term leases. The flip side is that most landlords don't want to give in to this request.

The reality is that major chains and anchor stores will get twenty-to-thirty year leases; ma-and-pa stores won't. Their lease will generally be on the order of three to five years. Shorter term leases are not necessarily that bad though.

Most landlords will offer a typical three-year lease deal with a provision for renewal after the term. This can actually be better for the start-up venture, especially if things begin to go wrong and you want to exit.

## Assignment and Subleasing

Make sure you have an assignment and subleasing clause in your rental agreement. This can be the greatest asset with regard to your exit strategy, whether you decide to sell or lease the restaurant to someone else. A well-written clause in this area can add goodwill to your store because it will appeal to potential buyers. Purchasers will be in essence buying the lease along with the fixtures.

Make sure that you have the option of removing equipment from the premises in the event you leave for whatever reason.

## Rent Escalation Provisions

Landlords like to use the consumer price index or CPI, which is the government's tool for measuring increases in key consumer goods. The rational is that they are due incremental increases in their service because of inflation, etc. Avoid these, if you can.

Major restaurant chains negotiate provisions in case of a downturn in business. You should be aware of this and ask for the same things, if possible. If there is a sudden downturn in business, you must have the ability to adapt. For example, what will you do if the highway department decides to refurbish the road in front of your store for six months? What would happen if there was a union strike of employees who were repaving the parking lot in front of your store? Be sure to include a clause in your contact that your rent will be reduced if these kinds of situations develop. These provisions can also protect you from acts of god, such as weather-related problems and war.

## Mitigation

Though not a leasing clause, mitigation is something that you should be aware of.

The landlord has a a responsibility to mitigate damages in the event that things don't work out according to the lease contract. For example, if you move out of your store on year three of a five-year lease the landlord can sue you for the remaining two years rent plus ancillary costs, such as broker commissions. However, if you move out and the landlord leases the vacated premises for what would have been the remaining two years on your lease, the landlord can't collect rent from the new tenant and collect rent from you. A landlord can't collect double rent. By law the landlord must mitigate, or lesson your damages.

# CAM, Taxes and Insurance

Listed below you will find a summary of highlights regarding CAM, taxes and insurance as they relate to retail leasing. The word "rent" in retail leases actually refers to four categories of income due to the landlord. They are:

- Rent.
- CAM.
- Taxes.
- Insurance.

We have discussed a couple rent provisions already: Percentage rent and per-square-foot rent. Now let's take a look at some other rent provisions. Each item may be billed separately or items may be combined, as the landlord sees fit. Most landlords choose to show the rent amount as "base rent", followed by any combination of CAM, taxes, and insurance. (CAM, taxes and insurance are also called triple net charges. These are basically pass-through charges for which you will be responsible.)

The most confusing category of expenses for the tenant is the CAM — No, this is not the engine part in your car. — Simply put, CAM costs are those costs associated with the maintenance and upkeep of the premises, and means common area maintenance costs, i.e. CAM. All tenants generally share in the common area costs and upkeep of the premises, such as landscape maintenance, driveway and parking lot maintenance; hence, the acronym CAM. The items covered in CAM are spelled out in the lease and are exclusively controlled by the landlord or his/her agent. Generally, the landlord will create a budget showing the expected annual expenses for the property. The tenants will then be required to pay their share in twelve equal monthly installments. No later than the first quarter of the following year, the landlord will furnish the tenants with a statement verifying the property's expenses for the year. At that time, the tenants are responsible to pay the landlord for their share of cost over and above the budgeted amount. In the event the landlord did not spend the entire amount, the landlord will give tenants a credit or refund the money.

Taxes and insurance are also part of CAM, but as explained earlier may be billed separately. However, these costs must be included in a tenant's review of total expenses because they are also administered and billed by the landlord.

Taxes are defined as the assessment on the real property (the land underneath the shopping center and all of its parts). Many tenants confuse these tax assessments with the tax due on their personal business property. However, the tenant is required to pay both assessments. It is customary for the landlord to allow the tenant to pay these charges monthly.

Insurance coverages placed by the landlord for the benefit of the center are also a part of CAM. Insurance premiums can also be reimbursed to the landlord on a monthly basis. Common types of coverage for a commercial facility are: Property coverage, liability, loss rents, or earthquake insurance. These coverages are in addition to the coverage the tenants must take out on improvements and equipment.

## Sample Lease Provisions

Below is a typical section of a retail lease, which provides an example of what has been explained so far.

**PRO RATA SHARE OF COMMON AREA EXPENSES, TAXES and INSURANCE:** Commencing the earlier of Tenant's opening for business or the Rental Commencement Date, Tenant shall pay to Landlord, as additional rent, one-twelfth (1/12th) of an amount reasonably estimated by Landlord to be Tenant's Pro Rata Share (as herein defined) of the total annual common area expenses, real property taxes and assessments and the costs of Landlord's insurance, as defined in Articles 5, 6 and 7, respectively, of this Lease; provided, however, the first month's estimated common area expenses, real property taxes and assessments and the costs of Landlord's insurance shall be payable by Tenant upon execution of this Lease. Tenant's Pro Rata Share shall equal the ratio of the total square feet of the floor area of the Premises to the total square feet of the floor area of all the buildings constructed and opened in the Shopping Center as of the end of each calendar year. Tenant's Pro Rata Share shall be subject to adjustment by Landlord to reflect Tenant's share of a particular cost that is not applicable to all the tenants within the Shopping Center. Landlord may adjust its estimate of such expenses at the end of any calendar quarter on the basis of Landlord's experience and reasonably anticipated costs. Following the end of each calendar year (and after the date of expiration or sooner termination of this Lease), Landlord shall furnish to Tenant a statement showing in reasonable detail the common area expenses, real property taxes and assessments and cost of Landlord's insurance during such calendar year (or portion thereof prior to the expiration or sooner termination of this Lease). If Tenant's share of such costs exceeds Tenant's payments so made, Tenant shall pay Landlord the deficiency within twenty (20) days after receipt of such statement. If such payments exceed Tenant's share of such costs, Tenant shall be entitled to credit the excess against payments for such costs next thereafter to become due Landlord as set forth above. Upon termination of this Lease, if Tenant is not in default hereunder, Landlord shall promptly refund to Tenant the amount of any excess.

**COMMON AREA**: Is defined as all areas and facilities within the Shopping Center not appropriated to the exclusive occupancy of tenants, including, but not limited to, all vehicle parking spaces or areas, roads, traffic lanes, driveways, sidewalks, pedestrian walkways, landscaped areas, signs, service delivery facilities, common storage areas, common utility facilities and all other areas for non-exclusive use in the Shopping Center which may from time to time exist. Common Areas shall include the roofs and exterior walls (other than storefronts) of buildings in the Shopping Center, all shared utility systems to the point of entry to any individual leased premises and all utility systems which are exterior to the buildings other than: (a) heating, ventilating and cooling system components or elements which serve individual tenants, and (b) sewer laterals to the point of junction with a common sewer line, which shall be the responsibility of individual tenant whose premises are serve by such lateral.

Common Area Expenses. The term "common area expenses" shall include, without limitation, all amounts paid by Landlord for the maintenance, repair, replacement, operation and management of the Common Area, including insurance covering the Common Area, together with an administrative fee equal to fifteen percent (15%) of all such amounts, and shall include, without limitation, the costs of gardening; landscaping; re-paving; resurfacing; re-striping; security; property management; repairs, maintenance and replacements of bumpers, directional signs and other markers; painting; lighting and other utilities; cleaning; common area trash removal; Tenant's trash removal (if contracted by the Shopping Center); depreciation and replacement of equipment; and the costs of public liability and all-risk property damage insurance covering the Shopping Center (including earthquake insurance, if purchased by Landlord).

Control of the Common Area. Landlord shall have exclusive control of the Common Area and may exclude any person from use thereof except bona fide customers and service suppliers of Tenant. Tenant acknowledges that Landlord may change the shape, size, location, number and extent of the improvements to any portion of the Shopping Center without Tenant's consent. Tenant and its employees and invitees shall observe faithfully and comply with the rules and regulations for the Shopping Center, and any amendments thereto or other reasonable rules and regulations governing the Shopping Center.

**TAXES:** The term "real property taxes" shall include, without limitation, any general or special assessment, tax, commercial rental tax, in lieu tax, levy, charge, or similar imposition imposed by any authority, including any government or any school, agricultural, lighting, drainage or other improvement or special assessment district, or any agency or public body, as against any legal or equitable interest of Landlord in the Premises and/or the Shopping Center or arising out of Tenant's occupancy of the Premises or which are attributable to the Premises, together with the reasonable costs of professional consultants and/or counsel to analyze tax bills and prosecute any protests, refunds and appeals for the period covered during the Lease Term. Tenant's liability with respect to such taxes and assessments shall be prorated on the basis of a 365-day year to account for any fractional portion of a fiscal tax year included in the Lease Term at its commencement or expiration (or sooner termination).

### INSURANCE; INDEMNITY; SUBROGATION

General. All insurance policies required to be carried by Tenant under this Lease shall: (i) be written by companies rated A-/ IX or better in the most recent edition of "Best's Insurance Guide" and authorized to do business in the state in which the Premises are located and (ii) name Landlord and any parties designated by Landlord as additional insured. Any deductible amounts under any insurance policies required hereunder shall be subject to Landlord's prior written approval, which shall not be unreasonably withheld. Tenant shall deliver to Landlord certified copies of its insurance policies, or an original certificate evidencing that such coverage is in effect, on the Term Commencement Date and thereafter at least thirty (30) days before the expiration dates of expiring policies. Coverage shall not be canceled or materially reduced (and the certificate of insurance furnished by Tenant shall verify same), except after thirty (30) days prior written notice has been given to Landlord's property administrator. Tenant's coverage shall be primary insurance with respect to Landlord and its property administrator, and the officers, directors and employees of both of them. Any insurance or self-insurance maintained by Landlord and/or its property administrator shall be in excess of, and not contributing with, Tenant's insurance. Coverage shall apply separately to each insured against whom a claim is made or suit is brought, except with respect to any aggregate limit applicable to the insuring party's policy.

Tenant's Liability Insurance. Tenant shall keep in force during the term of this Lease a policy of commercial general liability insurance insuring against any liability arising out of Tenant's use, occupancy, or maintenance of the Premises and the acts, omissions and negligence of Tenant, its employees, agents and contractors in and about the Premises and the Shopping Center. As of the Term Commencement Date, such insurance shall provide coverage for and shall be in the amount of not less than One Million Dollars ($1,000,000.00) per occurrence/Two Million Dollars ($2,000,000.00) aggregate for bodily injury and Property Damage. Landlord shall have the right to increase the amount of insurance required hereunder to reflect changing market conditions or industry standards. Tenant's coverage shall be primary insurance as respects Landlord, its officers, agents and employees. Any insurance or self-insurance maintained by Landlord shall be excess of the Tenant's insurance and shall not contribute with it. Coverage shall apply separately to each insured against whom a claim is made or suit is brought, except with respect to the limits of the insurer's liability.

Tenant's Other Insurance. Tenant shall maintain special form property coverage, with sprinkler leakage, vandalism and malicious mischief endorsements on all of Tenant's fixtures, including tenant improvements and betterment, equipment and personal property on the Premises, in an amount not less than one hundred percent (100%) of their full guaranteed replacement value, the proceeds of which shall, so long as the Lease is in effect, be used for the repair or replacement of the property so insured. Tenant shall maintain Worker's Compensation insurance in accordance with the laws of the state in which the Premises are located and employer's liability insurance with a limit of not less than One Million Dollars ($1,000,000.00) each accident. Tenant shall maintain plate glass insurance, sufficient to pay for the replacement of and any or all damages to exterior plate glass and storefront supports in the Premises. In the event Tenant sells alcoholic beverages from the Premises, tenant shall maintain a customary policy of liquor liability insurance with limits no less than those required above with respect to Tenant's commercial general liability insurance under previous section.

## Chapter Notes

# Design & Build-out

Design and build-out takes you into the process of setting up your store. It explains what is required in regard to permits and licenses. Here you will find an explanation of the different space configurations that most landlords offer. Finally, there is a restaurant construction guide that outlines all construction requirements with which you will need to be familiar.

The design and build-out of your restaurant depends on four major factors:

• The menu.
• Production requirements.
• Build-out configuration and aesthetic appeal.
• Government regulations.

## The Menu

Your menu will dictate the kind of production equipment that you will need. If you offer pizza, then you will need to have a pizza oven capable of baking the product to your requirements. If you offer speciality coffee drinks, like espresso, then you will need to have an espresso machine. Therefore, your menu will drive your equipment selection, and much of your build-out configuration.

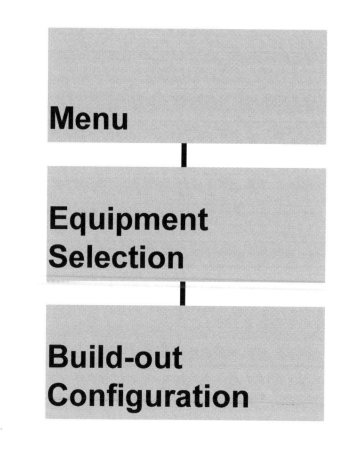

## Equipment Selection

Chapter 8, *Equipment*, discusses the sourcing of equipment, how to find it, and ways to finance it. For now, it is important for you to know that your restaurant equipment selection will have a direct bearing on how your store will be configured. For example, if you require a large walk-in freezer, space must be allocated for this, which will leave less space for other production equipment. As a general rule, start with the largest equipment, then work backwards to the smallest. Be sure to include tables and large sinks at the top of your list.

## Build-out Configuration

Planners use graph paper to get a general feel for restaurant layout. Once they know all the equipment that is needed to satisfy the menu requirements, they then get the physical dimensions and electrical requirements of the equipment. This information is available from manufacturers' brochures, equipment dealers, or by simply inspecting the actual piece of equipment. After they have these details, they cut out scaled plots of the pieces, to get an idea of a layout. The plots give a quick representation and can be easily moved to do "what if" comparisons. There are also specialized CAD (computer aided drawing) programs for this part of the work. They are sophisticated and will do a lot, however the learning curve is rather steep.

## Production Requirements

Production requirements are also driven by your menu, or more specifically the menu recipes. Just as your menu will dictate the kind of equipment that you will need, it will also dictate ancillary needs, such as dry food and supplies storage. If you have a Chinese take-out restaurant, your menu will drive the food storage area and the packaging storage area. As a take-out store, you will need to have storage space allocated for plastic cartons and containers.

Regardless of the type of restaurant, you can never have too much dry storage space. This is very often overlooked in planning because sales volume and inventory reorder points often are not addressed.

## Aesthetic Appeal

The decor, or aesthetic appeal of your restaurant, is the ambiance that you want to create for the customer. It has a direct bearing on your restaurant build-out configuration and expense. It involves things like, floor, wall coverings, and lighting fixtures - basically, anything that is designed around the equipment floor plan. For example, your restaurant may be Hawaiian-themed, and require grass-thatched roofs over the bar and eating booths. The floor may require special clay tile. And, there may be requirements for special coral lighting fixtures.

## Government Regulations

Government regulations will have a direct bearing on your restaurant design and build-out. See the construction guide for food facilities later in the chapter to get an idea of what is required here. Also, see Chapter 8, *Equipment*, which has some details about permits and government regulations and how they pertain to equipment. For now, be aware that this will affect the design and build-out of your store.

## Design Costs

Food facilities designers (FFD) can assist you in layout. These individuals have more experience than architects when it comes to restaurants. Most FFD designers have a minimum fee: $1,000 to $1,500.

| | |
|---|---|
| Basic design & layout | $1.00 per square foot |
| Basic design & layout w/permits | $2.50 per square foot |
| Architectural drawings | $500 to $700 |

The design work should include construction details and equipment layout. Architectural drawings will include store elevation and ceiling elevation.

Be sure to include the design costs as a line item in your start-up cost schedule.

## How long will it take to open a store?

If you are opening your first store, be prepared to spend some time on the project, it can take from six to eighteen months. This is another reason it's good to do all your planning on paper. Planning will reduce the amount of time it takes to open.

## Construction Build-out Costs

Costs for build-out for a new start-up will vary depending on the location of your store and the condition of the location. There are four basic scenarios:

- A brand new shell.
- A new vanilla shell.
- A former retail business.
- A former retail restaurant.

Be aware that the cost of remodeling an existing retail location can sometimes cost more than building out a new empty bay.

As a general rule, figure about $65 to $70 per square foot to do the construction for a vanilla shell with an ADA bathroom already in place. This includes plumbing for floor sinks.

A shell is basically a bay that has nothing in it. It might have some air-conditioning ducts, but that's about it; no ceiling; no electrical panel. A vanilla shell usually has an electrical panel in place, an Americans with Disabilities Act bathroom, and a plumbing main to tap into. However, there is no ceiling. If the site was a former retail business, it will have some fixtures, a bathroom and a ceiling. If the site is a former restaurant, it will have most improvements needed for a wrap store/juice bar operation, including floor drainage sinks required by county health departments. The sinks are placed in the floors to drain water from hand-washing and dishwashing sinks, and water runoff from equipment such as ice machines.

Before you sign a lease, negotiate your improvement costs because some or all of these costs may be paid for up-front by the landlord. Try to get them to amortize some/or all of the tenant improvement costs over the life of the lease. Tenant improvements are things such as remodeling, and construction related start-up expenses. If you negotiate these costs

**TIP**

*For more on lease negotiations, see Chapter 6,* **Leases & Negotiation**.

into your lease, you can save valuable capital resources at start-up.

# Construction Guide for Food Facilities

The construction guide presented here is intended to serve as a general overview of restaurant code requirements and should not be considered all inclusive. For specific code requirements in your region, contact the government agency in your area, which is usually your county health department or your local city.

You will be required to have all construction work conform to local city building codes. You will be required to obtain the necessary approvals from the local building and fire authorities prior to construction.

## Plan Check Fees

You will be required to submit a fee with your restaurant drawings. Plan check fees vary from region to region, but generally the fee is based on the size of your restaurant: Between $700 to $900, with 2,000 square feet being on the low side of the schedule.

## Remodels

A remodel is any construction or alteration to an existing food facility. Remodeling also includes the installation of equipment or repairs that alter a food facilities configuration or method of operation. Remodel does not include the following types of construction, which would be considered new construction:

• The installation of a food facility in a new structure, or in an empty building shell.

• The installation of a food facility in a former nonfood related facility, such as a shoe store, or in a former food facility from which all equipment and interior structures have been removed.

## Plan Submittal

Plans must be drawn to scale, i.e., 1/4" = 1', using non-erasable ink or print (no pencil), and must include:

1. A site plan showing the proposed rubbish and food waste storage receptacle location.

2. Complete floor plan with plumbing and electrical outlets and electrical panels.

3. Remodel plans must identify all proposed changes to existing structures, spaces, and equipment.

4. Complete equipment layout, including elevation of equipment and equipment specifications.

5. Complete exhaust ventilation plans including make-up air. (Indicate the type of comfort cooling in building, e.g. "building is cooled by refrigerated air conditioning", "evaporative cooling", or "no cooling system is installed".)

6. Finish schedule for walls, ceilings, and floors that indicates the type of material, the surface finish, the color and the type of integral coved base at the floor/wall juncture. Samples of proposed finish materials should be submitted with the plans.

7. A statement of the proposed customer-seating capacity when applicable.

8. Location of the manager's or chef's office. Spaces such as changing rooms or food storage cannot be used for office space.

Plans that are incomplete, and plans that have a multitude of changes will require revisions before approval may be granted. If any changes to the approved plans are proposed, they must be reviewed and reapproved by the governing agency prior to being implemented.

Approved materials and good workmanship are significant factors in the evaluation and final field approval of food facility construction and equipment installation.

All equipment design, construction and installation is subject to approval by the governing agency. National Sanitation Foundation (NSF) standards are used as a guide for equipment evaluation and approval, except where strict compliance with the NSF standards is a specific requirement.

## Field Construction Inspections

### Preliminary Inspection

When construction is approximately 75% to 80% complete, with plumbing, rough ventilation, and rough equipment installed, you must call the plan checker assigned to review your plans for a preliminary construction inspection. Requests should be made at least two (2) working days in advance. In no case should a preliminary inspection be scheduled for less than two weeks prior to the proposed opening of the food facility.

### Final Inspection

Upon completion of the construction, including all finishing work, you must call the plan checker assigned to review your plans to arrange for a final construction inspection. You will not be issued a health permit until the facility passes a final inspection. Contact your plan checker at least two (2) working days in advance for an appointment for the final inspection. Final construction must be approved by the governing agency prior to opening for business or use of remodeled areas.

## Construction and Equipment Requirements

The plans must show and specify in detail the following:

1. Floors:

a) Floors in food facilities (customer area floor requirements are less stringent) shall be smooth and impervious to water, grease, and acid, and of easily cleanable construction. Floor surfaces in all areas where food is prepared, packaged, or stored, where any utensil is washed, where refuse or garbage is stored, where janitorial facilities are located, in all toilet and handwashing areas and in employee change and storage areas, shall be an approved type that continues up the wall or toe-kicks, at least four (4) inches, in a seamless manner, forming a 3/8 inch minimum radius cove as an integral unit. Topset base is generally not acceptable, except in dining areas and areas where food is stored in its original shipping container.

b) Floor drains are required in floors that are water-flushed for cleaning, where pressure spray methods for cleaning equipment are used, where slip resistant agents are used on floors and where excessive moisture may accumulate, such as in food processing plants. Where floor drains are utilized, the floor surface shall be sloped 1:50 to the floor drains.

c) High pressure hot water cleaning systems are required in addition to floor drains if the degree of roughness of the slip resistant agent is deemed excessive upon evaluation by this Agency.

d) Flooring under equipment and on the coved bases shall be completely smooth. Floor surfaces which contain slip resistant agents shall be restricted to traffic areas only.

2. Walls:

a) Walls in food preparation areas and dishwashing areas shall be smooth and

b) nonabsorbent, with a light colored, easily cleanable finish. (Note: Brick, concrete block, rough concrete, or rough plaster are not acceptable.)

c) Materials other than smooth plaster or putty coat plaster, drywall with sealed and taped joints or plywood with properly sealed joints require submission of sample.

d) All surfaces shall be sealed with a gloss or semigloss enamel, epoxy, varnish, or other approved sealer.

e) Other wall surface materials are subject to evaluation and compliance with the same or similar requirements prior to installation.

f) Wall surface requirements in customer areas are less stringent.

3. Ceilings:

a) Ceilings in kitchen food preparation areas shall be smooth and nonabsorbent, with a light colored, washable finish.

b) Acoustical tile may be approved if it complies with the preceding requirements and if a sample is submitted and approved.

c) Acoustical plaster is not an acceptable ceiling finish in the food and utensil handling areas.

4. Conduit:

a) All plumbing, electrical, and gas lines shall be concealed within the building structure to as great an extent as possible. Where this is not possible, all runs shall be at least 1/2 inch away from the walls or ceiling and six (6) inches off the floor.

b) Where conduit or pipe lines enter a wall, ceiling or floor, the opening around the line shall be tightly sealed.

c) Conduit or pipe lines shall not be installed across any aisle, traffic area, or door opening.

d) Multiple runs or clusters of conduit or pipe lines shall be furred in, encased in an approved runway or other sealed enclosure approved by this Agency.

5. Exhaust Hood and Ducts:

a) Mechanical exhaust ventilation shall be required at or above all cooking equipment such as ranges, griddles, ovens, deep fat fryers, barbecues and rotisseries to effectively remove cooking odors, smoke, steam, grease, and vapors.

b) All hoods, ducts, and exhaust outlets shall be installed in accordance with Chapter 20 of the current edition of the Uniform Mechanical Code as adopted by the local building department.

c) All joints and seams shall be tight or soldered for ease of cleaning. Riveted seams are not acceptable.

d) Food heating or warming devices, cheese melters, etc., that are installed above other equipment beneath an exhaust hood may create an air flow obstruction to proper ventilation of the basic equipment for which the hood ventilation system is designed. The design, construction and installation of such warming devices under a hood are subject to evaluation and approval prior to installation.

e) Canopy-Type Hoods: The lower lip of canopy-type hoods shall not be more than seven (7) feet above the floor and shall not be more than four (4) feet above the cooking surface. The hood shall overhang or extend a horizontal distance not less than six (6) inches beyond the outer edges of the cooking surfaces, on all open sides. It shall have grease troughs and drip pans that are easily cleanable.

f) Noncanopy -Type Hoods: Noncanopy-type hoods will be approved providing they are constructed to be easily cleanable and they comply with the minimum exhaust air velocity requirements. Shielding at the ends of the hood may be necessary to prevent interference from cross drafts.

g) Make-Up Air: Make-up air shall be provided at least equal to that amount which is mechanically exhausted. Windows and doors shall not be used for the purpose of providing make-up air.

h) Fire Extinguishing Systems: Fire extinguishing systems may be required by local fire department codes. They shall be installed so as to allow easy cleanability of the hood and duct systems, and whenever possible, shall not be installed above food or utensil handling areas.

6. Refrigeration:

a) All refrigeration units shall be adequate in capacity to the needs of the proposed operation and shall comply with the following requirements:

1) Be capable of operating so as to maintain the refrigerated foods at or below 45 degrees Fahrenheit at all times.

2) Be specifically constructed for commercial use (domestic model refrigeration units will not be accepted - Must be NSF approved).

3) Be provided with an accurate, readily visible thermometer.

4) Have shelving that is nonabsorbent and easily cleanable.

5) Have smooth, nonabsorbent and easily cleanable surfaces. If cement, plywood, or other similar absorbent materials are used, the surfaces must be sealed. All joints must be sealed.

6) Condensate waste from reach-in refrigeration units may be drained into a floor sink or an approved evaporator unit.

7) Cooling coils and related electrical, drainage and refrigerant lines shall be installed in a safe and easily cleanable manner. Drainage and refrigerant lines shall be constructed of nontoxic materials or properly insulated and covered with an approved, easily cleanable and nontoxic material.

8) Ice Machines: All ice machines shall be located within the building in an easily cleanable, well-ventilated area, and shall be drained to a floor sink.

b. Walk-in Refrigeration Units shall also:

1) Have an integrally coved base with a radius of at least 3/8 inch at the floor/wall juncture; the floor material shall extend up to a height of at least four (4) inches on the walls. Four (4) inch approved metal topset coving with a minimum 3/8 inch radius is acceptable against metal wall surfaces of walk-in refrigeration units. Samples of flooring materials must be submitted for approval by this Agency prior to installation.

2) Open into an area with approved finishes within the facility. Refrigeration units may not open into the customer area or directly outside, with exception of customer self-serve prepackaged refrigeration units.

3) Have shelving that is at least six (6) inches off the floor with smooth, easily cleanable legs, or cantilevered from the wall, for ease of cleaning. Small, easily movable, castered dollies may be used in place of a lower shelf inside a walk-in refrigeration unit.

4) Have condensate waste drained into a floor sink. The floor sink is not to be located inside the walk-in refrigeration unit.

## Floor Sinks

a) All condensate and similar liquid waste shall be drained by means of indirect waste pipes into an open floor sink.

b) Floor sinks shall be installed flush with the floor surface.

c) Horizontal runs of drain lines shall be at least 1/2 inch from the wall and six (6) inches off the floor and shall terminate at least one (1) inch above the overflow rim of the floor sink.

d) Floor sinks shall be located so that they are readily accessible for inspection, cleaning, and repair. The floor sink must be located within 15 feet of the drain opening of the equipment served.

e) Waste lines may not cross any aisle, traffic area, or door opening.

f) Floor sinks or floor drains are not permitted inside walk-in refrigeration units.

## Kitchen Utensil Sink

a) Where multiservice kitchen utensils (i.e., pots, pans, etc.) are utilized, there shall be provided at least a two-compartment stainless steel sink with dual, integrally installed stainless steel drainboards.

b) A separate, approved two-compartment sink must be installed within each department in a grocery store which handles unpackaged foods, i.e., deli, meat, bakery, etc., and satellite food service facilities in restaurants, i.e., sushi bars, oyster bars, etc.

c) The minimum compartment sizes shall be at least 18" x 18" x 12" deep with minimum 18" x 18" drainboards, or 16" x 20" x 12" deep with 16" x 20" drainboards, (The sink must otherwise be capable of accommodating the largest utensil to be washed, and the drainboards shall be as large as the largest sink compartment.)

d) When a sink is installed next to a wall, a metal "backsplash" extending up the wall at least eight (8) inches shall be formed as an integral part of the sink and sealed to the wall.

## Eating and Drinking Utensil Sink

a) Where multiservice eating and drinking utensils are washed by hand, (see exception when a dishmachine is used) a three-compartment stainless steel sink with dual, integrally installed stainless steel drainboards shall be provided. The three-compartment sink may replace or be in addition to the required two-compartment sink.

b) The minimum compartment sizes shall be at least 18" x 18" x 12" deep with minimum 18" x 18" drainboards, or 16" x 20" x 12" deep with 16" x 20" drainboards, (The sink must otherwise be capable of accommodating the largest utensil to be washed, and the drainboards shall be as large as the largest sink compartment.)

c) When a sink is installed next to a wall, a metal "backsplash" extending up the wall at least eight (8) inches shall be formed as an integral part of the sink and sealed to the wall.

## Automatic Dishmachines (Dishwashers)

a) All automatic dishmachines must be listed by NSF or be equivalent.

b) All spray type dishmachines which are designed for a hot water sanitizing rinse shall be provided with a booster heater that meets the requirements of NSF Standard No. 5, or be connected to an approved recirculating water system which is capable of maintaining the rinse water at not less than 180 degrees Fahrenheit.

c) The dishmachine must also be provided with thermometers and pressure gauges to indicate the proper water flow pressures and temperatures. Appropriate valves for testing the accuracy of the gauges and thermometers shall also be properly installed.

## Garbage Disposals

Garbage disposals are not required. When a garbage disposal is installed, it may be installed in a drainboard if the drainboard is lengthened to accommodate the disposal cone in addition to the minimum required drainboard size. Garbage disposals may not be installed under a required sink compartment unless an additional compartment is provided for the disposal.

## Janitorial Sink

a) A one-compartment, wall-mounted janitorial sink with hot and cold running water shall be installed for general cleanup activities. Cement tubs are not acceptable.

b) A curbed area properly sloped to a drain, that is provided with hot and cold running water, a mixing faucet, and an approved backflow prevention device, is also acceptable. All curbed area surfaces shall be of smooth, impervious, and easily cleanable construction. Where duckboards or floor mats are used, a curbed area with a drain is required.

c) Free standing janitorial sinks must be provided with NSF type easily cleanable legs. Legs with "L" angles will not be accepted.

## Handwashing Sinks

a) Handwashing sinks shall be provided in the food preparation areas.

b) Soap and sanitary towels shall be provided in single-service, permanently installed dispensers at all handwashing sinks.

c) A separate, approved handwashing sink must be installed within each department in a grocery store which handles unpackaged food, i.e., deli, meat, bakery, etc., and satellite foodservice facilities in restaurants, i.e., sushi bars, oyster bars, etc.

## Food Preparation Sinks

Food facilities that prepare raw vegetables or meat may be required to have a food preparation sink. This sink must have an indirect connection to a floor sink.

## General Purpose Hot Water

a) Provide a water heater which is capable of constantly supplying hot water at a temperature of at least 120 degrees Fahrenheit to all sinks, and other cleanup facilities. In sizing the water heater, the peak hourly demands for all sinks, etc., are added together to determine the minimum required recovery rate.

b) A water heater should *not* be purchased until the health department determines the minimum required size for the food facility.

## Dipper Well

A running water dipper well must be provided if scoops are used for dipping ice cream. The dipper well shall be drained by an indirect connection to a floor sink.

## Window Screens

All openable windows, such as restroom windows, shall be screened with not less than 16-mesh screening.

## Unpackaged Foods

Displays of unpackaged foods shall be shielded so as to intercept a direct line between the customer's mouth and the food being displayed, or shall be dispensed from approved self-service containers. (Request the health department's policy memorandums for detailed requirements regarding sneezeguards, buffets, salad bars, and bulk food operations.)

## Dry Food and Beverage Storage

a) Adequate and suitable floor space shall be provided for the storage of food, beverages, and related products. In addition to working storage and refrigeration storage, additional backup storage must be provided. Working storage is considered to be cabinets over and under food handling equipment and wall-mounted shelves which are located in and used in conjunction with food preparation areas. Reference the following to determine the minimum amount of backup storage space which will be required:

1) Within food facilities that have food preparation areas which total 400 square feet or less and have 100 customer seats or less, a minimum 100 square feet of floor space shall be dedicated for backup dry food storage. At least 32 linear feet of approved shelving units shall be installed in the 100 square feet of dedicated floor space.

2) Within food facilities that have food preparation areas which total more than 400 square feet, or more than 100 customer seats, the floor space required for backup dry food storage shall be determined by dedi-

cating one square foot of floor space per customer seat, or by dedicating a space equal to 25% of the food preparation area, whichever is greater. The quantity of shelving units to be installed in this dedicated space shall be based upon whichever of the following formulas provides the greater amount of shelving:

(a) Required linear footage of shelving units =

$$32 \text{ x (seating capacity)} / 100$$

(b) Required linear footage of shelving units =

$$32 \text{ x (sq.ft. of preparation areas)} / 400$$

3) Each department in a grocery store which handles unpackaged foods, i.e., deli, meat, bakery, etc., must provide at least 32 linear feet of approved shelving units.

4) Within produce departments of grocery stores or produce stores (produce only), a segregated room or area with at least 50 square feet of floor space shall be dedicated for backup storage of food and packaging supplies. At least 16 linear feet of approved shelving units shall be installed in the 50 square feet of dedicated floor space.

5) Within bars/taverns, a segregated room or area with at least 50 square feet of floor space shall be dedicated for backup beverage and bar supply storage. At least 16 linear feet of approved shelving units shall be installed in the 50 square feet of dedicated floor space. When a bar is located within a restaurant, the backup storage requirement for the bar must be provided in addition to the required backup dry food storage.

6) Satellite or remote food service operations in restaurants, such as sushi bars and espresso bars, must provide at least 16 linear feet of approved shelving units.

b) A shelving unit shall be a minimum 18 inches in depth and three tiers high. For example, eight shelving units, each of which is four feet long and three tiers high would equal 32 linear feet of shelving units.

c) Shelving shall be constructed in an easily cleanable design of smooth metal or wood which has been finished and sealed. Shelves installed on a wall shall have at least one (1) inch of open space between the back edge of the shelf and the wall surface, otherwise, the back edge of the shelf shall be sealed to the wall with silicone sealant or equivalent. The lowest shelf shall be at least six (6) inches above the floor, with a clear unobstructed area below or be the upper surface of a completely sealed continuously coved base, with a minimum height of four (4) inches. All shelves located below a counter or work surface shall be set back at least two (2) inches from the drip line of the surface above. If shelves are supported by legs on the floor, the legs shall be smooth and easily cleanable.

d) Electrical panels, large fire prevention system components, or similar wall-mounted equipment shall not be installed in food storage rooms unless adequate approved provision is made to compensate for the space required for the installation.

## Restrooms

a) Toilet facilities shall be provided within each food facility convenient for the employees.

b) If there are five or more employees, separate toilet rooms for each sex shall be provided. Local building departments or Alcoholic Beverage Control may require two restrooms regardless of the number of employees.

c) Toilet facilities shall be so situated that patrons do not pass through food preparation, food storage, or utensil washing areas when they are allowed access to the toilet facilities.

d) The floors, walls, and ceiling shall have surfaces that are smooth, non-absorbent, and easily cleanable.

e) Handwashing sinks shall be provided within each toilet room. The sink shall be provided with hot and cold running water from a mixing type faucet. Soap and sanitary towels in single-service, permanently installed dispensers shall be provided at the handwashing sink.

f) Toilet tissue shall be provided in a permanently installed dispenser at each toilet.

g) The restrooms shall be provided with tight-fitting, self-closing doors.

h) All toilet rooms shall be provided with ventilation. If adequate ventilation cannot be provided by an openable, screened window, mechanical ventilation will be required.

## Clothing Change Rooms

a. Change Rooms

1) A room or enclosure, at least 4' x 5', separated from toilet, food storage, or food preparation areas, shall be provided where employees may change and store their outer garments and personal belongings. A larger change room or rooms may be required, depending upon the total number of employees.

2) The clothing change room may not be used as an office.

3) No telephone jacks, computer jacks, water heaters, or other appurtenances will be accepted in this room.

b. Designated Areas

1) A designated area may be substituted for a change room if the facility has less than five employees per shift.

2) The designated area must be physically segregated from toilet rooms, food storage areas, food preparation areas, and utensil washing areas by approved partitions or walls.

3) Within the designated area, one locker (minimum 12" x 18" x 36") per employee on a given shift must be provided.

## Pass-thorough Windows

a) When food is passed through a window to a customer on the outside of the building, the size of the window opening may not exceed 432 square inches.

b) The minimum distance between pass-through windows is 18 inches.

c) All openings must be equipped with a sliding closure device (e.g. glass, screen). This device must be kept closed except when food is being passed out to the customer.

d) The counter surface of the pass-through window must be smooth, free of channels and crevices, and be easily cleanable.

e) The pass-through window shall be equipped with an insect exclusion device which will produce an air flow eight inches thick at the discharge opening and an air velocity of 750 feet per minute as measured three (3) feet below the device. The air flow must continue along the entire horizontal width of the window opening. If the pass-through window opening is less than 216 square inches, an insect exclusion device will not be required.

## Delivery Doors

a) All delivery doors leading to the outside shall open outward, be self-closing, and shall be provided with an overhead insect exclusion device. The air curtain, when installed inside the building, must produce a downward-outward air flow not less than eight inches thick at the discharge opening and with an air velocity of not less than 750 feet per minute across the entire opening as measured at a point three feet above the floor. The device shall turn on automatically when the door is opened. When installed outside the building, the same velocity of air must be directed straight down over the entire door opening.

b) Large cargo-type doors shall not open directly into a food preparation area.

c) An insect exclusion device is not a substitute that would permit a door to remain open.

## Customer Entrance Doors

a) All customer entrance doors leading to the outside shall open outward, be self-closing and be provided with overhead insect exclusion devices or other effective means to prevent the entrance of insects. Refrigerated, positive pressure air conditioning with all doors self-closing is another acceptable method (except at delivery doors). The insect exclusion devices must produce a downward-outward air flow not less than eight inches thick at the discharge opening and an air velocity of not less than 750 feet per minute across the entire opening as measured at a point three feet above the floor. The device shall turn on automatically when the door is opened.

b) An insect exclusion device is not a substitute that would permit a door to remain open.

## Garbage and Trash Area

a) An area shall be provided for the storage and cleaning of garage and trash containers.

b) The walls, floor and ceiling of this room or area shall be constructed so as to be smooth, imperious, and easily cleanable.

c) Outside trash storage areas should be situated as far away from delivery doors as possible.

## Lighting

a) All food preparation areas, all dishwashing areas, and all bar and fountain glass washing sinks (except where alcoholic beverage utensils are washed), shall be provided with at least 20 footcandles of light, as measured 30 inches above the floor.

b) Food and utensil storage rooms, refrigeration storage, toilet rooms, and dressing rooms shall be provided with at least 10 footcandles of light.

## Equipment

a) All show and display cases, counters, shelves, tables, refrigeration equipment, sinks, and other equipment used in connection with the preparation, service and display of food, shall be made of nontoxic materials and so constructed and installed as to be easily cleanable.

b) All equipment shall be placed on minimum six (6) inch high, easily cleanable legs or on a four (4) inch high continuously coved curb, or on approved casters, or cantilevered from the wall in an approved manner.

## Water and Sewage Disposal

All liquid waste, including sewage, generated by a food facility, shall be disposed of in an approved manner into either a public sewer system or to an approved private on-site sewage disposal system.

## Americans with Disabilities Act

The Americans with Disabilities Act (ADA) became federal law in 1990. It prohibits discrimination against individuals with disabilities in employment and mandates their full participation in both publicly and privately provided services and activities. The ADA requirements became effective on July 26, 1992, for employers with 25 or more employees; and on July 26, 1994, for employers with 15 or more employees.

The ADA requires that public accommodations, such as restaurants, retail stores, hotels, theaters, doctors' offices, pharmacies, private schools, and day care centers, may not discriminate against persons with disabilities. Reasonable efforts must be made to remove existing barriers and new construction must be accessible.

The law is complex and wide ranging in regards to ADA, and cannot be briefly summarized here. For information call The Equal Employment Opportunity Commission (EEOC): 800-669-3362. They publish The ADA - Your Responsibilities as an Employer.

# Equipment & Layout

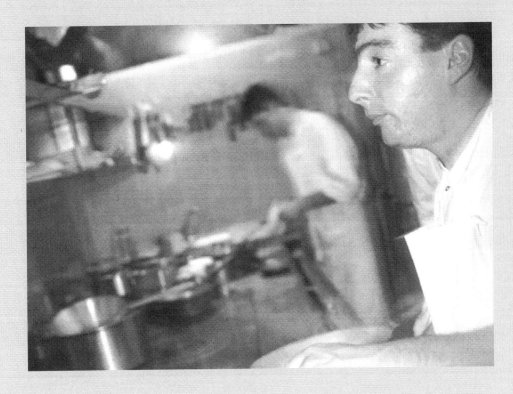

T his chapter explains what you need to know about store equipment. Some of the topics include: government regulations, sources for equipment, buying and leasing considerations, and equipment lease negotiations.

# Equipment

The kind of equipment that you will need for your restaurant will be predicated on the food and beverages that you will be preparing. A bar or night club will have different equipment requirements then a fast-food restaurant. Therefore, it is important to plan your menu in advance of your equipment acquisitions because the menu will dictate the equipment.

## Government Regulations

There are generally two government agencies that you will deal with when setting up your restaurant:

1. The health department.
2. The building department.

To find out what type of equipment you'll require, one of the first places to start is the local health department, or the government agencies responsible for inspecting and passing business establishments that serve the public. The government has specific requirements that need to be addressed. For example, you might find requirements for employee dressing rooms and lockers, special types of sinks, specific requirements for hot water temperature and flow, etc. All of the requirements vary from region to region. Therefore, it is important to check with these entities early in your planning process.

The health department will deal with specific requirements in regard to health safety, specifically, consumer health, and the health of your employees.

The building department will be concerned about the structural and general safety aspects. For example, they will make sure that all the electrical wiring is up to code and that all the inspections are done for each phase of the construction project.

Once you know what is needed to pass the health inspection, you can begin to take the proper steps to get things moving. If you have chosen a location that was previously a restaurant, determine what will have to be done to bring the establishment up to current construction codes. To find this information go to the local city or county building department, which deals with construction codes. Depending on how long the previous location was vacant, new codes may or may not be enforced. Sometimes the older codes are *grandfathered*, meaning that the older codes can be used. Be sure to check this out in advance because it can save you a lot of money it you don't have to meet new codes. If you're going to build a new facility, you'll have to meet current health codes.

## Permits and Licenses

Government agencies will charge for their services in the way of permits, licenses, or fees. The health department will want a health inspection fee. The building department will want plan check fees. For example, you will need to submit your architectural drawings to the building department and then wait for them to approve them. Once they approve the plans, then - and only then - start the build-out of your restaurant. Likewise, the health department will require you to submit plans that show basic floor and wall covering specifications, the location of floor sinks, and the location of all equipment. *Check the heading, Construction Guide For Food Facilities, on page 7.6, for specifics.*

When obtaining restaurant equipment, you basically have the following options for buying, financing, or leasing:

1. New equipment.
2. Used equipment.
3. New and used equipment.

## Primary Sources for Equipment

Local restaurant and bar equipment dealers can supply you with brochures and price lists. The restaurant business is a local business. Therefore, you should establish a relationship with a local equipment dealer right away. Dealers sell new and used equipment. A visit to a well-stocked dealer can be a real eye opener. Plan to visit several early on in your planning stages. Most manufacturers of restaurant equipment have dealer networks; however, in today's high-tech world, it is simple to get information directly from the Internet. To find a local equipment dealer, simply go to the yellow pages in your local phone book. Look under the headings: *Restaurant equipment* or *rental - restaurant*.

*You can get contact information for suppliers at the Web site.*

## Secondary Sources for Equipment

Finding used restaurant equipment is not that difficult. You can search local newspaper want ads to see what is available, or log onto the Internet. For example go to *www.recycler.com* or go to online auctions Web sites like ebay, *www.ebay.com*. Talk to other bar and restaurant owners about equipment; you'll be surprised how much equipment is stashed away in the back, in storage, or in the garage at home.

If you go the used-equipment route, you can save a considerable amount of your valuable start-up cash. However, be aware that used equipment is sold as-is. If you don't have the technical capabilities yourself, be sure to have a technician check out your potential purchase before you buy. You don't want to get stuck with a lemon.

Visit restaurant locations that you aspire to. Talk to the people at the location. You'll be surprised at how much information they will share with you. People love to talk about themselves and their business. This may sound tacky, but go through their trash. It's amazing what you will find there in the way of resources!

Local restaurant auctions are another source for equipment. In fact, auctions are where many dealers buy their used stock that they refurbish and resell. You will usually have an opportunity to inspect the equipment prior to the auction. However, you may not be able to operate the equipment because it may be in a location that does not have electrical power readily available. For example, you might find a three-door freezer in the back of a warehouse. It may look great, but there won't be any way to "fire it up" before the auction. The age-old term buyer beware holds true here. Most local auctions will have a preview one to three days before the auction to give you time to evaluate the merchandise.

## Buy or Lease

Buying a piece of equipment will almost always be less expensive then leasing. For example, if you lease an ice machine for $100 per month for 36 months, your total lease payments would equal $3,600. Contrast this with the purchase price of $2,200.

You have the option of leasing or buying equipment. If you lease used equipment, the leasing company will purchase it and lease it back to you. There are advantages either ways. With purchasing, you at least have the asset on your financial statements, even if you have loan payments. With leasing, you have a fixed monthly cost for all your equipment. This can have an advantage because you won't have to come up with heavy down payments for purchases, which can save money at start-up. However, you won't have the asset because you won't own the equipment. One major reason for leasing equipment is to protect yourself from product obsolescence. Computers are popular lease items because their productive lifetime diminishes quickly. Therefore, many companies lease this kind of high-tech equipment. Leasing rather than buying equipment can help start-ups and established firms alike move forward without tying up working capital.

The advertising phrase "Buy now, pay later" sometimes fools people into thinking that they can get something for next to nothing.

Business owners who lease equipment have a strategy designed to help them manage their venture without tying up money needed for working capital. Therefore, leasing can help a firm by enabling it to conserve capital, keep pace with technology, and expand its purchasing power.

According to the U.S. Department of Commerce, 30% of all equipment purchases include leasing, and four out of five companies lease some or all of their equipment.

Although there can be drawbacks to leasing because interest rates are generally higher than those for bank financing, and some leases can limit a business's ability to borrow further, the practice is still widespread.

As mentioned, many start-ups lease equipment. One important aspect of the lease is the maintenance contract. Will you be responsible for the equipment if it fails? Make sure that they will maintain and repair the equipment. For example, many beverage suppliers will rent you a beverage dispensing system and they will also maintain it if you buy the beverage products from them. They may offer you product pricing terms whereby you may pay a little more for the product thereby paying for the lease of the equipment. This can be a real lifesaver when a piece of equipment fails during a busy restaurant shift.

New leased equipment should carry a typical service agreement, which is the warranty offered to cover any manufacturer's defects or malfunctions in the equipment. Any leased equipment should carry these warranties, the same as if the equipment were purchased outright.

A maintenance contract is a contract over and above the original service agreement. Usually it is not necessary unless the equipment is the kind that needs frequent calibration and cleaning, such as beverage dispensing equipment or espresso machines.

A lease contract can take many forms, depending on the type of equipment leased and the length of time it is needed. With many leasing agreements, payments are tax-deductible, which could mean a larger tax break for the business if the value of the equipment were depreciated.

## Types of Leases

Lease terms vary from simple month-to-month, to complex. You can rent an ice machine for a monthly flat rate or you might opt to lease the machine on contract for thirty-six months, which is the standard in the industry. However, the longer-term leases usually have termination clauses and other provisions that can cost you if you want to vacate the lease before the lease matures.

To determine which pieces of equipment to lease, pick units that cost more than $3,000. These durable assets, which are things that will last for years, lend themselves to leases best.

With operating leases, which are the principal types of leases, payments don't show up on the balance sheet as debt, so they don't affect the company's ability to borrow further. Operating-lease payments commonly expire before the end of the expected useful life of the equipment, and they include a premium to compensate the leasing company for assuming the risk of obsolescence of the equipment.

Although payments on capital leases generally are lower than those on operating leases, they show up on a company's balance sheet as debt, which may limit the firm's ability to borrow.

A company can lease almost any kind of business equipment. Leasing is especially appropriate for companies whose equipment, (computers, for example) likely will become obsolete quickly.

## The Leasing Process

Whatever the form of the leasing contract, it is a type of borrowing, so there is interest to be paid, usually at a fixed rate. As a rule the effective rate of interest on a lease is higher than that for commercial bank financing--often 18 percent or more.

Like commercial banks, leasing companies look at the creditworthiness of the business, and often of the business owner. The lease applicant should be able to provide company and personal financial statements as well as a business plan detailing the equipment needed, its purpose, and the revenues it is expected to produce.

Start-ups usually finance most of their costs with their own funds and outside capital, and use lease arrangements for some equipment. If the lease is approved, the leasing company buys the equipment from the manufacturer and leases it for a specific period, passing along financing costs and sometimes other costs connected with the deal. Interest rates on leased equipment are often higher for start-ups than for established companies because of the associated risk, and negotiating power of the established companies, which are usually chain restaurants.

## Where The Lessors Are

Leasing companies operate throughout the United States, offering everything from telephone systems to turnkey manufacturing operations.

As mentioned before, a good source for leasing are major restaurant equipment dealers. They usually have relationships with banks, finance companies, and independent leasing companies

Hundreds of independent leasing companies do business in urban and rural areas alike. Check the Yellow Pages under *leasing services* or *equipment leasing*. Many restaurant equipment dealers also have the ability to work lease deals. Be sure to ask when you contact them.

Many equipment manufacturers offer leasing services through subsidiaries to help market their products. Also, a number of companies offer lease arrangements for equipment made by other manufacturers.

Most major banks also offer leasing services to businesses of all sizes. For a general discussion of leasing, visit the site of the Equipment Leasing Association of America, at *www.elaonline.com* The site has sections on why businesses lease, the types of leases available, and how leasing works

## Equipment Lease Negotiation

Be sure you have an idea of the terms of the lease. Longer leases, 48 month and 60 month, may have lower lease payments, but may cost you much more in the long run.

Make sure the lessor shows you the total that you will be paying over the life of the lease, not just the monthly payment. This will protect you from inflated payments that go over the dollar amount that you agree to at the start of the lease.

Leases are legal contracts, so be sure to read them. As, with any contract, the terms may be subject to negotiation. So, once you read the contract, ask if specific provisions can be changed. For example, there may be a section that states that you will be responsible for paying a flat rate service fee of $75 every time a technician visits. Ask to have this removed and try to negotiate the best deal you can get on a maintenance contact.

Leasing can be a benefit to you. However, take this decision seriously, because the risks may outweigh the benefits. And above all, read the fine print!

## Equipment Selection

More than likely the government agency issuing you a health permit to operate will require that all of your restaurant production equipment be NSF certified.

The National Sanitation Foundation, or NSF, is an independent, not-for-profit organization providing a wide range of services around the world. NSF concentrates is on food, water, indoor air and the environment. NSF develops national standards, and provides third-party conformity assessment services

The Food Equipment Program begins with voluntary standards that represent a consensus between manufacturers, users, and regulatory authorities. The registered NSF Certification Mark on a food equipment product confirms that NSF has assessed its conformity with the relevant standard. As part of the certification process, the production facility is audited annually. The purpose of this audit is to assure that all the requirements of the standard continue to be met, quality assurance and quality control procedures are followed in fabrication, products are sampled and retested on schedule, and labeling and product literature are true and accurate.

All approved restaurant equipment will display the NSF certification label sticker. The sticker is tamper-proof; damage to the sticker will void the certification. Therefore, the first thing to look for when selecting a piece of equipment is the NSF certification label. You might find a great deal on a used piece, only to find out later that you can't use it in your store because it is not certified. Here is what the label sticker looks like:

If you do not have the necessary technical background to evaluate a used piece of equipment, you are much better off buying from a reputable restaurant equipment dealer. They normally only buy NSF-certified equipment for refurbishing and resale. You will pay more for used equipment at a dealer; however, you will have the piece of mind that the equipment is certified. Also, dealers usually offer warranties with their products. This can provide you with even more added support.

*See the section*
***Construction***
***Guide for Food***
***Facilities***, *in*
*Chapter 3, for*
*more details on*
*plan require-*
*ments.*

## Equipment Layout

Restaurant equipment layout is an art and is best left up to a professional food facilities planner. A good planner will save you money in the long run and his/her breadth of experience will be worth every cent.

The layout sketch will give you a basic idea how a typical shopping center bay can be configured. The rule of thumb is the one-third rule, whereby the entire store is divided into thirds: Customer area, food preparation area and storage, and personnel.

### One-Third Rule

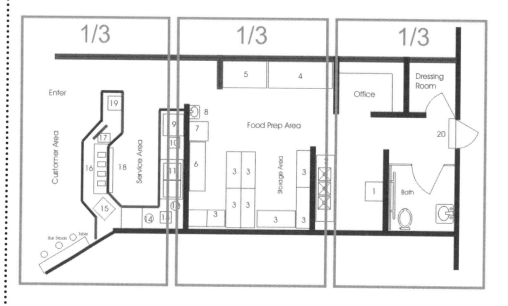

Note the numbered items on the drawing above. These reference the numbers on an equipment list. The number 3 pertains to wire shelving, and the number 4 pertains to a stand-up freezer. This layout is representative of the kind that you will need to show the local health department in order to receive a health permit.

# Financing Your Restaurant

This chapter offers you a quick overview of some of the sources where you might find financing for your store. From partners, family, friends, government loan programs, to credit cards, this chapter offers strategies to help you get the start-up capital.

# Money Sources

Where are you going to get the money to start your restaurant?
Will you:

- Provide the money yourself from savings or existing equity?
- Take a loan from a bank or the government?
- Get a loan from friends and family?
- Provide an equity stake in your business to business partners?
- Credit cards?

There are many ways to approach the financing of your venture. I will
discuss a few of them here. Keep in mind that you can use a combination
of these when exploring the financing of your store.

## You Have The Money

By far, the easiest way to obtain money to start your store is to provide it
yourself. You might have savings that you can dip into, or you may have
property with equity that you can use to borrow against. You may want to
consider providing some of your savings and the rest in a loan. For example, you could provide half your start-up capital from your savings and
the other half from a property equity line.

Property equity lines are relatively easy to get these days. Basically, these
are secured loans that are based on the value of your property. For example, if you paid $100,000 for your house and the appraised value is
$125,000, you could borrow $25,000, which is the equity that you have
built in the property over time. The bank protects itself by securing the
loan. This means that if you do not pay back the loan, the bank can fore-
close on your property and force the sale of the property to pay back the
loan.

## The Bank Has The Money

The reality is that most banks will not loan you money unless you have
collateral that they can use to secure a loan. You can't blame them. They
are in business too, and must protect their interests. You can dress up in
your Sunday suit and take your spit-polished business plan into a meeting
and try to convince a banker to loan you all the money to start your venture. However, be ready for rejection.

There are two factors that bankers have been conditioned to when it comes to financing restaurants:

1. They generally do not make loans for restaurants because there is no collateral stake that they can make. For example if loans are not repaid, they know that the value of used equipment goes down fast. So, if they had loaned you money based on the new market price, they would be in the hole if they had to sell the assets to pay for delinquent loans.

2. They have been conditioned by stories of restaurant failures and that restaurants change hands often. The industry just does not have a good reputation when it comes to financial ratios, like income-to-debt ratios. If bankers can't get their measurements around your idea, they will not invest in it.

## The Government Has The Money

The United States Small Business Administration (SBA) might invest in your idea by providing you with a loan. However, they generally provide business planning assistance through associations like their Small Business Development Centers and The Service Corps of Retired Executives (SCORE). The government has grant money available; however, qualification parameters are constantly changing. To get an idea of what is available go to the Small Business Administrations Internet Web site at *www.sba.gov.*

## Family and Friends Have The Money

Family and friends can be a good source for funds. As long as you treat these sources with respect and show them your plans, you may find an early supporter in your quest for start-up capital. Keep all business relationships professional, even if family and friends are involved.

Many personal relationships can be destroyed if there was no attention paid to the business side of the relationship. If someone loans you money, sign a note of promise to pay, with the specific terms of repayment set fourth in the note. This will make for a better relationship overall because you will be showing your friend and/or family member that you are a responsible business person.

## Partners

Many people form partnerships to assist in the financing of a business and to help share and limit risk. Working partners generally have a say in how the business is run; silent partners do not. There are many ways to set up partnerships. For example, in order to maintain decision control of your company, you can elect to have silent partners, whereby they will be provided an equal share of the ownership of the business in exchange for their investment.

## Credit Cards

In today's credit-happy society, banks are eager to provide credit cards to almost anybody. Once you establish good credit through the credit bureaus, the banks will be sending you unsolicited applications with lines of credit and generous repayment interest rate terms. Credit cards are basically unsecured lines of credit, meaning that there is no collateral needed to obtain them. Interest rates can be higher than more conventional loans; however, they can help with some of your start-up expenses when establishing your store. As with any loan, be sure to include these loan expenses as part of your start-up expense.

## Your Plan of Attack

Keep in mind that financing your business is going to be one of the most difficult aspects of starting up. It is going to demand that you establish your credibility and integrity with people. Creativity can be your key to success in regard to how you choose to approach loans from banks, government, friends, and partners.

Your business plan is your critical success tool. Your plan will tell prospective investors what your concept is and what you are all about. Don't be shy. Show your plan with pride. When asked a specific question, say, "...let's see what page that is on...", and turn to the specific page in your business plan. Once you do this, the demeanor of your prospect will change immediately.

Establish your credibility by sharing with your prospect your professional background and why you are convinced your business concept will work. Be enthusiastic and knowledgeable about your goals.

## Constructive Criticism

Listen and adapt. Bankers, friends, and family might offer suggestions about how you can improve your pitch for a loan. If they do, don't get defensive. Instead adapt your business plan and loan pitch to deal with their objections. The main element in your proposal is selling. You are selling yourself and your ideas. In order to successfully close the sale, you will need to deal with all of the prospects objections.

Obtaining funds for your restaurant can be a daunting task. It can be a time-consuming and sometimes frustrating project. However, with persistence and organization you will prevail.

## Chapter Notes

# Management & Operations

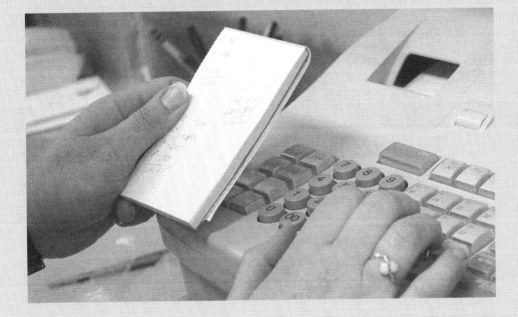

This chapter will introduce you to critical techniques that will help you manage your store. I have concentrated on aspects that you will need to be familiar with before you open. Topics covered include: Menu design, supplier selection and sourcing, hiring techniques, employee evaluation techniques, employee shift scheduling, and employee policies.

# Management Techniques

## Hiring

The purpose of the first part of this chapter is to teach you a method that can be used to quickly and easily convert subjective information into objective information. This will provide you with a decision-making tool that can be used in a number of different ways to quantify information.

You will learn a technique that can be used to evaluate potential job candidates. Some of the benefits of this technique are:

- Improves clarity in any selection process.
- Removes subjective bias from decision-making process.
- Provides excellent feedback.
- Eases modification.
- Saves time.

## Evaluation of Potential Job Candidates

Often the selection process for hiring is left to a manager's subjective bias. All managers have fallen victim to making hiring decisions that have come back to haunt them; basically, because they made a bad decision based on their personal preferences, rather than on specific objective criterion. A bad decision is costly because it wastes time, resources, and could result in unnecessary legal action.

### Definitions

- **Subjective** - Of or resulting from the feelings of the person thinking rather than the attributes of the objective thought of; imaginary or biased.

- **Attribute** - A characteristic or quality of a person or thing. A quality, gift or talent.

- **Objective** - Existing as an object or fact independent of the mind. Real, unbiased.

# Weighting-Scoring Model

A weighting-scoring model allows an objective overview of subjective information. It allows you to weight specific criteria, or rank the importance of criteria. Score the criteria, then, total the scores. The score range is 0-5.

## Definitions

• **Criteria** - A standard, rule, or test by which judgment can be formed. A yardstick or guideline.

• **Weight** - An assignment of importance, priority, or ranking for criteria.

• **Score** - A rating for each criterion. A tally or count.

| Kitchen Evaluation Weighting-Scoring Model | | | | | | | |
|---|---|---|---|---|---|---|---|
| CRITERIA | WEIGHT | \multicolumn{5}{c}{SCORE} | TOTAL |
| | | 1 | 2 | 3 | 4 | 5 | |
| 1. Dishwasher | 40% | | | | | X | 2.00 |
| 2. Microwave Oven | 10% | | | | | | 0.00 |
| 3. Dual Oven | 40% | | | X | | | 1.20 |
| 4. Large Window | 10% | | X | | | | 0.20 |
| GRAND TOTAL SCORE | 100% | | | | | | 3.40 |

For example, the above chart shows four criterion for the selection of the ideal kitchen that can be used while shopping for a house. Someone else's criteria might be different. Each specific criteria is weighted by a percent. In this case, the dishwasher is most important as evidenced by its weight of 40%. The dishwasher in this house got a top score of 5, meaning that it is what the shopper was really looking for; however the window, got a low score of 2. There was no microwave oven, therefore the score of 0.

The overall score for this kitchen is 3.40. When one of these forms is filled out for each house that is visited, a profile and reference can be quickly established for each location. The shopper will have all the information and scores when he/she finally gets down to deciding which house to buy  - and with that perfect kitchen!

This same method can be applied to potential job candidates.

## Job Candidate Evaluation

### Step 1 - Establish Specific Criteria

As in the kitchen example, you will need to establish your grading criteria for the job. Each job has different criteria. For example, a manager position would have different criteria than a service clerk. However, some of the criteria might be the same. You might choose to test both the manager and the service clerk on their cash register experience by having them actually operate a cash register. Then, you would record the score of the test on the weighting-scoring model that you created.

The hiring criteria for our example job, service counter person, is displayed below.

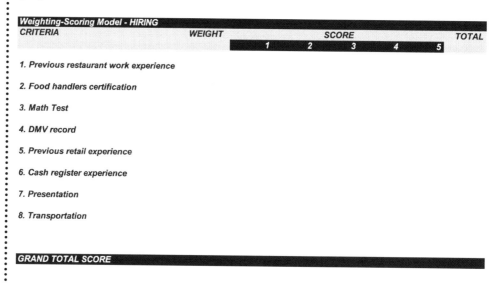

| Weighting-Scoring Model - HIRING | | | | | | | |
|---|---|---|---|---|---|---|---|
| **CRITERIA** | **WEIGHT** | **SCORE** | | | | | **TOTAL** |
| | | 1 | 2 | 3 | 4 | 5 | |
| 1. Previous restaurant work experience | | | | | | | |
| 2. Food handlers certification | | | | | | | |
| 3. Math Test | | | | | | | |
| 4. DMV record | | | | | | | |
| 5. Previous retail experience | | | | | | | |
| 6. Cash register experience | | | | | | | |
| 7. Presentation | | | | | | | |
| 8. Transportation | | | | | | | |
| **GRAND TOTAL SCORE** | | | | | | | |

You can develop any criteria that you wish. The important thing is to measure what you develop, so that you will know where you are in relation to your ultimate goal of hiring a qualified person for the job

## Step 2 - Weight Specific Criteria

This is where you rank the criteria that you have selected. You weight the criteria in regard to importance. For example in our model, criteria 1, "Previous restaurant experience", received a weight of 25%, while "Previous retail experience" received a weight of 15%. Both have a higher weight in relation to the other criterion, because it is assumed that job candidates who have had previous experience will possess many of the necessary skills that we desire: Customer relations experience, cash register experience, food handling experience, etc.

Once you have established weights for each criteria, you can now begin

| Weighting-Scoring Model - HIRING | | | | | | | |
|---|---|---|---|---|---|---|---|
| CRITERIA | WEIGHT | SCORE | | | | | TOTAL |
| | | 1 | 2 | 3 | 4 | 5 | |
| 1. Previous restaurant work experience | 25% | | | | | | |
| 2. Food handlers certification | 10% | | | | | | |
| 3. Math Test | 5% | | | | | | |
| 4. DMV record | 15% | | | | | | |
| 5. Previous retail experience | 15% | | | | | | |
| 6. Cash register experience | 5% | | | | | | |
| 7. Presentation | 10% | | | | | | |
| 8. Transportation | 15% | | | | | | |
| GRAND TOTAL SCORE | 100% | | | | | | |

the interview process and gather the necessary information to complete your model.

## Step 3 - Gather Information

The information that you will need to score job candidates, will come from the application for employment and any test(s) that might be administered. You can verify work experience simply by calling the previous employers listed on the application for employment. Test results can easily be computed once a test has been administered. To save time, a simple math test can be administered at the same time a candidate fills out the application for employment.

Once all the information has been gathered, it is time to score the job candidate.

## Step 4 - Score the Candidate

Scoring is the final stage of the process. Utilizing all the information that we have gathered from step 3, we simply fill out the "score" section of our weighting-scoring model.

Our example candidate received high scores for criteria numbers: 1,2,7,8. She scored a 4 on our math test, and scored a 3 on criteria 4, DMV (Department of Motor Vehicle) record.

**Weighting-Scoring Model - HIRING**

| CRITERIA | WEIGHT | SCORE 1 | 2 | 3 | 4 | 5 | TOTAL |
|---|---|---|---|---|---|---|---|
| 1. Previous restaurant work experience | 25% | | | | | X | 1.25 |
| 2. Food handlers certification | 10% | | | | | X | 0.50 |
| 3. Math Test | 5% | | | | X | | 0.20 |
| 4. DMV record | 15% | X | | | | | 0.45 |
| 5. Previous retail experience | 15% | | | | X | | 0.60 |
| 6. Cash register experience | 5% | | | | X | | 0.20 |
| 7. Presentation | 10% | | | | | X | 0.50 |
| 8. Transportation | 15% | | | | | X | 0.75 |
| **GRAND TOTAL SCORE** | **100%** | | | | | | **4.45** |

We would most likely hire this job candidate because she scored high on our criteria.

## Evaluating Employee Performance

Here is a simple three-step process to help evaluate employee job performance. The steps are:

• Create a results-oriented job description
• Develop a weighting-scoring model.
• Use weighting-scoring model to evaluate employee.

### Step 1: Creating A Results-Oriented Job Description

Many job descriptions are poorly written. They are vague. They do not establish specific goals, and do not convey the most basic information to the employee. Consequently, there is a gap in basic perception about what a manager and employee view as the job from the very beginning of the business relationship. This can create doubt and apprehension, which can destroy a partnership. We can clarify this situation by creating a results-oriented job description.

Start by specifying the major job functions, or duties, for the job.

*Job Description = Job Functions + Tasks*

• Specify each job function under the "Functions" heading.
• Under the "Primary Duties and Responsibilities" heading, list each job function that you specified - The function now becomes a goal that can be measured.
• Under each job function, list general tasks to successfully accomplish each function.

In the example position description - titled number 1 on the next page - for the Service Counter Person. Note that each function is in simple sentence form in the Functions heading; then, repeated again under the Primary Duties and Responsibilities heading as numbered line items. This format presents the functions as numbered goals and then specifies the tasks, indicated with letters, needed to accomplish the goals.
Linking the tasks that must be accomplished to complete the functions, as goals, is the key to creating a results-oriented job description.

### K.I.S.S.

Many of you are probably familiar with the acronym, K.I.S.S., which stands for *Keep It Simple Stupid*, a term used by business people. The simpler you make a job description, the more clear and concise it is. The difficult part is breaking the job down into its least common elements. Most managers have a tendency to load a job description with everything they can think of. This approach creates clutter that can overwhelm an employee.

**Weighting-Scoring Model**

File: wsm_manual_form.xls

| CRITERIA | WEIGHT | SCORE | | | | | TOTAL |
|---|---|---|---|---|---|---|---|
| | | 1 | 2 | 3 | 4 | 5 | |
| 1. Maintains high level of customer service & customer awarness | | | | | | | |
| 2. Works primary service and food prep area | | | | | | | |
| 3. Maintains store appearance | | | | | | | |
| 4. Participates in continuous improvement activities | | | | | | | |
| 5. Assists in promotion activities of store | | | | | | | |
| 6. Maintains accurate inventory records | | | | | | | |
| 7. Assists in opening and closing of store | | | | | | | |
| 8. Participates in other activities | | | | | | | |
| 9. Attendance | | | | | | | |
| **GRAND TOTAL SCORE** | | | | | | | |

2

1

## POSITION DESCRIPTION

**TITLE:** Service Counter Person

**REPORTS TO:** Store Manager

**FUNCTIONS:** Maintains high level standard of customer service and customer awareness. Works primary service area and primary food prep area. Maintains store appearance. Participates in team efforts to constantly improve customer service and improve efficiency of operations. Assists in promotion activities of store. Maintains accurate inventory records. Assists in open and closing of store. Participates in other activities.

## PRIMARY DUTIES AND RESPONSIBILITIES

1. **Maintains high level of customer service and customer awareness**

This will be accomplished by:
   a. Greeting each customer with an enthusiastic "Hello".
   b. Directing "New" customers to the Menu area.
   c. Answering customer questions in a prompt courteous manner.

2. **Works primary service area and food prep area**

This will be accomplished by:
   a. Following specific procedures, written and verbal, for: Product preparation, product delivery, and cash register operations.

3. *Maintains store appearance*

This will be accomplished by:
   a. Constant diligent effort to maintain hygiene standards as outlined by civil health codes. Following specific directives for cleaning: Service area, prep area, customer areas, both inside and outside, and public restrooms.
   b. Maintaining store uniform to provide daily smart, clean, appearance.

Note how simple the example job description is. It has been broken down into simple understandable language and clear attainable goals. A rule of thumb: In general, a job description should be no more than two pages.

## Break Bread

Have the employee participate in the creation of his/her job description. Ask an employee: What is your job? Have the employee write down, in his or her own words, what he or she does on the job. Chances are, it will be different than what the formal job description is (assuming a formal job description has been created). It is amazing what you can learn by giving an employee an opportunity to do this.

You can motivate an employee by reassessing his or her job description. Simply, incorporate some of the points you discovered when you had the employee write his or her own job description. Hold a meeting with the employee and explain that you want to rewrite the job description utilizing the employee's input on some issues. This is a major selling point for the job description because it gives you, the manager, the opportunity to break bread with the employee. When all is said and done, both the manager and the employee should sign the job description, which solidifies the job description as a contract.

## Step 2: Develop a Weighting-Scoring Model

All too often managers are faced with evaluating their employees with techniques that are old and outdated. Many companies use standard canned employee evaluation forms, which are usually purchased directly from stationary stores or office supply houses. These canned forms have nothing to do with the employee's specific job functions. The assumption is that they will work fine for any type of job, whether the job is lawn care or sheep ranching in Colorado.

Employee evaluation is an ongoing periodic process - and should not be considered a dreaded annual managerial process, which is typical in most organizations. Employees need constant feedback to perform their jobs effectively.

## Procedure

- Develop weighting-scoring model. Functions from job description become scoring criteria for this model.
- Develop a model for manual processing.
- Develop a computer model to tabulate the total scores. This can be for any time frame. We have found the best model is an annual model with quarterly reviews.

It is easy to create an employee evaluation weighting-scoring model directly from a job description because the functions in the job description become the scoring criteria for the model. Simply transfer the function information from the job description right into the model as exemplified in our example (titled 2 on the previous page). Now you must determine the importance of the criteria.

Specifying the importance of the criteria is the weighting portion of the weighting-scoring model. Basically, you assign a weight of importance to each criteria, which in turn denotes the criteria rank. In our example, we weighted the criteria, Maintains store appearance at 25%. This criteria had more weight of importance applied to it than, Attendance, which is weighted at only 15%. Therefore, in this example, a clean store is ranked, or weighted, 10% higher than employee attendance. As a rule of thumb, weight your criteria using percentages that total 100%.

**Employee Evaluation Weighting-Scoring Model**

| CRITERIA | WEIGHT | SCORE | | | | | TOTA |
|---|---|---|---|---|---|---|---|
| | | 1 | 2 | 3 | 4 | 5 | |
| 1. Maintains high level of customer service & customer awarness | 5% | | | | | | |
| 2. Works primary service and food prep area | 15% | | | | | | |
| 3. Maintains store appearance | 25% | | | | | | |
| 4. Participates in continuous improvement activities | 10% | | | | | | |
| 5. Assists in promotion activities of store | 10% | | | | | | |
| 6. Maintains accurate inventory records | 5% | | | | | | |
| 7. Assists in opening and closing of store | 10% | | | | | | |
| 8. Participates in other activities | 5% | | | | | | |
| 9. Attendance | 15% | | | | | | |
| **GRAND TOTAL SCORE** | **100%** | | | | | | |

## Step 3 - Score Employee Performance

Now all we have to do is fill out our model and calculate. First score the employee on each of the criteria. Then, multiply the score by the weight. Finally, add the individual totals to get the grand total score.

It is easy to create a weighting-scoring model using your favorite spreadsheet program. You can even create a quarterly spreadsheet and evaluate each employee on a periodic basis, rather than just once a year.

| Employee Evaluation Weighting-Scoring Model | | | | | | | |
|---|---|---|---|---|---|---|---|
| CRITERIA | WEIGHT | SCORE | | | | | TOTAL |
| | | 1 | 2 | 3 | 4 | 5 | |
| 1. Maintains high level of customer service & customer awarness | 5% | | | | X | | 0.2 |
| 2. Works primary service and food prep area | 15% | | | | X | | 0.6 |
| 3. Maintains store appearance | 25% | | X | | | | 0.5 |
| 4. Participates in continuous improvement activities | 10% | X | | | | | 0.1 |
| 5. Assists in promotion activities of store | 10% | | | X | | | 0.3 |
| 6. Maintains accurate inventory records | 5% | | | | | X | 0.2 |
| 7. Assists in opening and closing of store | 10% | | | X | | | 0.3 |
| 8. Participates in other activities | 5% | | | X | | | 0.1 |
| 9. Attendance | 15% | | | | | X | 0.7 |
| GRAND TOTAL SCORE | 100% | | | | | | 3.1 |

# Menu Design

Restaurant operators have an average of three minutes to impress customers with their menus. Make your best impression by creating a menu that markets your restaurant effectively. Menus should be graphically exciting, but first and foremost they should be functional.

Menu designs vary as much as restaurants do. Quick-service restaurants usually have bright back-lit menu boards that are directly behind the service counter personnel. In contrast, many fine-dining restaurants have menus printed on heavy expensive bond paper.

Menus are designed to accomplish four main objectives:

• List the food available.
• Define the concept and operation.
• Align the customer's expectation with the experience.
• Perform as a powerful marketing tool.

How well a restaurant's menu carries out these functions can determine customers' ultimate satisfaction, and a restaurant's total financial success.

Experts concede that many menus do not fulfill their function because they are poorly designed. The average customer spends about three minutes looking at a menu. If the menu does not reinforce the restaurant's objectives, than there is a missed opportunity to entice customers to spend their hard earned cash.

## Develop Your Menu Offerings

The first step in putting together a menu is developing your food-and-drink offerings. To attract customers, keep quality standards high. Restaurateurs and chefs search for a strategic menu mix that maintains the delicate balance between innovation and tradition, healthfulness and indulgence, delicacy and robustness.

Successful restaurants are those that keep up with the current food trends. Keep in step with what's selling and what's not, and then make the necessary adjustments. By analyzing the menu portfolio, slow selling items can be dropped in favor of trendier foods.

Customer surveys are a good way to find out what people like in order to get a better handle on customer response to a restaurant's menu. Simply ask them what they like, and what they don't like.

Every effort should be made to ensure that the item ordered is the most profitable one on the menu and that the menu itself shows your food — and your restaurant — in the best possible light. A good menu will sell, it will make patrons hungry, and if they can't decide among three different items, you have a better chance of getting them to return.

Your market niche will help define your menu. It's better to specialize than try to be something for everybody. You will get feedback from customers, but be aware of where you are at all times. It is best to aim for the norm within your customers. That is, find the consensus within that group, and then offer what they want.

Creating a successful menu can mean more than appealing to customer tastes. It is important to design a menu mix while being aware of the following production concerns:

- Ingredient shelf-life.
- Redundant ingredients.
- Seasonal availability of produce.
- Cooking methods.
- Sales, price, and labor.
- Physical space and inventory control methods.

## Menu Analysis & Food Costing

Many independent and chain restaurants have not done their food costing because it takes so long to do. However, don't overlook this important step or it could spell disaster for your restaurant.

You can create a menu sales mix analysis, which is designed to gauge each item on your menu. The system divides the menu items into four categories. The goal is to identify what your menu items are in relation to these names; then apply a specify strategy to market each one. There is a spreadsheet file available at the Web site that you can download.

The software program has been offered in the public domain and was adapted by David V. Pavesic, Ph.D., CHE, FMP with the programming assistance of Computer Information Systems masters students, Nicholas

Yu and Pinaki Mitra. The program is an example of how practical operations knowledge and computer technology can come together and create a management tool. It combines practical restaurant menu sales mix analysis data with computer technology utilizing Microsoft Excel 97 and Visual Basic for Applications. I'd like to thank these professionals for their efforts in the adaptation of this program and for unselfishly providing the program to the public.

## Menu Sales Mix Analysis Program Overview

*Get this computer program from the web site.*

The purpose of the software is to provide restaurant and food-service managers with a tool to analyze their menu sales mix. Point of sale technology (POS) allows operations to track the sales of every item on their menu (See section later in this chapter) to determine the popularity, cost, revenue and profit of each item. The data is usually displayed in spreadsheet format. While the information provided in the spreadsheet format is useful, the graphing of the spreadsheet data can provide even more detailed information to management.

The program allows the operator to categorize sales not only by meal period, but by menu categories, e.g., appetizers, side orders, entrees, desserts, and miscellaneous. Alcoholic beverages are categorized by spirits, beer, wine, liqueurs, and miscellaneous. The categories are viewed separately and then combined in a summary spreadsheet providing cost information that can be compared to figures reported on the monthly income statements.

There is graphing provided for each menu item relative to the mid points for food cost percentage, number sold (popularity), individual menu item gross profit, and average weighted gross profit by menu item allowing the operator to utilize three of the most widely used menu analysis perspectives, specifically, Cost/Margin Analysis (Pavesic), Menu Engineering (Smith and Kasavana) and the Miller Matrix (Miller).

With the inclusion of the technology of Visual Basic for Applications, the entire program is menu driven such that after entering only three bits of information on each menu item, namely the item food cost, its menu price, and the number sold, with the click of the mouse the data is automatically converted into a twenty-three column spreadsheet, which is then converted to graphs in any of the three menu analysis methods.

Once the sales analysis program has classified your menu items into one of the four categories for Cost/Margin, Miller Matrix and Menu Engineering, a strategy for improving or optimizing their overall impact on the menu sales mix can be put into action. The characteristics of the menu items will point you in the direction of what specific strategy would be best.

## Menu Strategies

Primes, Winners and Stars are popular, low food cost, and high weighted and/or individual contribution margin items. You want to sell more of these items than any others. Therefore, you should place these items in prominent positions on the menu and use menu psychology techniques to make them stand out to increase the likelihood of the guest noticing them and increase the possibility that they will be selected. Use techniques such as bold and oversized lettering, placing a box around the menu item, featuring it on a menu board, table tent, or having the server suggest it.

Maintaining high visibility is recommended for any menu item that is classified as a Prime, Winner or Star. It is very important to keep quality of ingredients high and portions adequate because these menu items are very likely house specialities or signature items that are specifically sought by customers. Because they are popular, you might even test for price elasticity - customers sensitivity to changes in prices - and increase the price if you feel it is low relative to competing items on the menu, especially if an item this popular is one of your lowest to moderate price items in its respective menu category. Be sure to monitor quality and presentation to ensure high standards on these items.

Plow horses are items that are popular and high in cost. With these items, test for price elasticity by raising prices on the items with the highest food cost percentages. This is an option especially if the item is one of your house specialties. If raising the price is not an option, consider reducing the portions or number of accompaniments. Portion reduction is not an option if the item is a 6-ounce filet, however.

If you can't raise the price or reduce the portion size, position the item in a less noticeable location on the menu to lower its selection odds. You may want to emphasize another item that is lower in food cost and higher in contribution margin. Food cost can also be lowered by finding a supplier who has a lower price on the key ingredients. If an item contains one or more expensive ingredients, you might have your chef develop a similar item that is combined with a low-cost ingredient, e.g., pasta or rice, and promote that item. Also, promote Sleepers and Puzzles to soften the high cost aspects of popular Standards and Plowhorses.

Sleepers, Low Volume-Low Cost Marginals and Puzzles would likely be Primes, Winners and Stars if you could increase their popularity with customers. These items are slow-selling items with low food cost. Therefore, anything you do to increase the likelihood that these items are selected by the guest should be tried: Prominently display them on the menu; feature them on your table tents and menu boards; have the server suggest them. Since they are very low in food cost, you can lower the price via discounts or early bird specials to stimulate sales. Also, increase portions or accompaniments to create a better value at a low price to stimulate sales. You may even be able to rename an item and promote it as a signature item.

Problems, Losers and Dogs are items that are unpopular, high in food cost. One of the first things you should consider doing is increasing the price; also lower the product cost. Examine the characteristics of the menu item. Is the quantity over-sized in terms of portion size and accompaniments? If so, cut back on quantities to reduce costs. If you cannot do either, hide it on the menu. Develop a substitute item and promote it. Combine with inexpensive ingredients to lower the product cost. If these things do not help, consider removing it from the menu completely.

The placement of menu items, the graphics and the item descriptions all send messages about what you want customers to order. You can draw attention to a menu item by, putting a box around it, or including an illustration of it and/or write lengthy copy about it. Place the item in a menu 'sweet spot' — either the top of a column or the top right-hand side of the menu. Place the high-end specialties on the inside right page, toward the middle. The more you bring attention to these items, the more you will sell.

Don't be too quick to eliminate less-profitable items, such as plow horses or chase those dogs off your menu. You can simply down play them instead. To minimize an item, remove boxes, remove copy and place it in a not-so-sweet spot. The item will still be on the menu, and the customer will still have access to it.

## Menu Layout

The goal of your menu should be functionality. However, it should also be used as an advertising tool because it can help win customers. Creative menu layout can help.

By using things like borders, illustrations, symbols, and heavier type, you can bring attention to menu items; however be careful not to overdo it. Use an easy-to-read typeface in 12-point size. The font you use, the size of print, boxes, shading and graphics all help draw attention to an item.

Photos seem to be effective for casual restaurants like coffee shops as well as for restaurants where customers might not be familiar with the foods.

Menu copy is an important aspect. As a general rule, a menu should not describe common, familiar items that customers know about. Save the space for describing your speciality items and selling high-margin items, like appetizers.

## Food Costing & Price

Managers should cost out each menu item before setting the price. Knowing the food cost is just a starting point. Restaurateurs often take their cost and multiply it by three or so to set their menu price. In other words, they aim for a food-cost percentage of about 33 percent of gross sales. Using this philosophy, an operator might be more apt to push an item with a 25 percent food cost than one with a 40 percent food cost. But that's just one ingredient to pricing. Another aspect is the actual profit margin on each item.

Focus on the profit, not the food-cost percentage for determining what to sell. Take the example of a restaurant that sells a $17 steak with a 40 percent food cost, netting a $10.20 profit, and a $11 chicken with a 25 percent food cost, netting a $8.25 profit. Even though the steak has a higher food-cost percentage, it still brings in $1.95 more per order.

············

# Purchasing & Inventory Control

The simple clerical act of buying supplies has been elevated to a purchasing function over the years. The same is true for inventory control. In fact, you can now get a college degree in these fields.

## Purchasing

When you start your restaurant, you will need to purchase equipment. This section deals with specifying and ordering primarily food and beverage products, which are items you will need to produce your products.

The purpose of a purchasing system is to ensure an uninterrupted supply of food, beverages, and other supplies at the best possible cost. This sounds easy. In practice, however, when you consider the relationships of demand, seasonalitity, lead times, transportation costs, shelf life, perishability, storage cost and inventory control costs, purchasing can begin to look more complex. This all points to the need for solid planning. Basic questions must be answered:

• What food and beverage products are needed?
• What quantities are needed?
• Who will supply the products at the best price with the best terms?
• What will be the frequency of order placement?
• When will deliveries be made?
• How will deliveries be made?
• Where and how will merchandise be stored?

### Selecting Products for Purchase

The menu dictates what food items need to be purchased. This, along with sales forecasts, can provide information for ordering. However, before you can order, you must have a specification of what to order.

Specifications are needed to communicate with your supplier. Their use can help avoid potential disputes about what is ordered and what is ultimately received. Specifications should state precisely the name of the product and all of its primary characteristics: Size or count, shape, color, texture, weight, density, moisture content, fat content, smell and packaging requirements.

Since many food products vary in size, shape, weight and color, it is important to specify the exact quantity that will comprise a measuring unit. For example, specify the exact number of shrimp in a pound. Specify the weight of chickens that you are ordering. Below is a sample product specification.

## Product Specification

**1. Item:** Yellow Corn

**2. Description:** Canned product prepared from clean, mature, discrete kernels by washing and shucking.

**3. Packaging:** Product shall be packed in #10 tin cans, six per corrugated case. Corrugated case to have minimum bursting strength of 250 pounds.

**4. Labeling:** All cans and cartons shall have legible characters and conform to all government regulations.

**5. Special Instructions:** U.S. Grade A product required. Heat-treated for proper preservation in sealed cans. Uniform size and color and per grade A specifications. Product consistency should be firm.

You should have a detailed specification for everything that you order. This will take time up front, especially during start-up, but the effort will be worth your time in the long run. Once you have everything specified, calling up product specification sheets from your files or database will be easy.

## Inventory Management

Inventory is the lifeblood of your business. A dime ingredient can put you out of business if you do not have adequate supplies on hand. You have to know what to buy and when to buy it.

The essence of inventory management can be summarized in three questions:

1. How much of a specific item should we purchase?
2. When should we buy a specific item to replenish our stocks?
3. How should we store our stocks until they are used?

The goal of an inventory system is to fulfill two major functions:

1. The inventory should provide customers with an assortment of products.
2. The system should cover normal sales.

## Economies of Scale

In many situations it is easier and more economical to deal in volume. It makes more sense to order a case of canned corn rather than order the cans one-by-one. The purchased quantity is referred to as the economic order quantity (EOQ).

The economic order quantity model determines the number of items to purchase that will minimize the combined costs of ordering and the inventory carrying cost. Ordering costs are the total operating expenses associated with purchasing: Placing direct purchase orders, followup, receiving department costs, and expenses incurred paying invoices. These total costs are divided by the total orders per year to arrive at the ordering cost per order. Carrying cost is the total of all expenses involved in maintaining inventory and includes expenses related to: cost of capital tied up in inventory, space charges, handling charges, insurance costs, spoilage and property taxes on unsold inventory.

$$EOQ = \text{The Square Root of } (2YS / IC)$$

Where $Y$ equals the annual sale of the item, $S$ equals the ordering cost per order, $C$ equals the unit cost of the item, and $I$ equals the carrying cost as a percentage of cost. For example, when an item sells for $1,200 per year and the ordering costs and the costs of lost sales due to stockouts are $75 per order, carrying costs are 25 percent and the item costs $6, the economic order quantity would be:

$$EOQ = \text{The Square Root of } (2 \text{ X } 1200 \text{ X } 75 / 0.25 \text{ X } 6)$$

Therefore, the EOQ = 346

This example is greatly simplified. There are several variations on the EOQ formula that take into account other variables such as product discounts and lead times. The goal is to show you how the different relationships interweave. With the advent of point of sale (POS) and inventory control computer software, this kind of function is performed easily.

**Inventory Turnover**

When 100 percent of your original inventory has been replaced, you have "turned over" your inventory. In general, the higher the inventory turnover, the better. The rule of thumb for the restaurant industry is three times per month.

Turnover = Cost of food consumed / average inventory

Cost of food consumed = (Beginning Inventory + Purchases) - Ending Inventory

Average inventory = Average of Opening and Ending Inventory

If you divide the turnover rate into 30 days, it will give you the number of days supply you are averaging in your inventory at any given time during the month.

Another way to calculate turnover is by measuring sales per square foot. Basically, once a month count the inventory in your restaurant. Then, calculate the inventory in dollars:

Inventory in Dollars = Average Sales / Square Footage

This method is predominantly used by retailers who have dedicated product shelf space, such as department stores.

## Safety Stocks and Uncertainty

If all inventory estimates and assumptions were realized in practice, then efficient inventory management would be relatively easy. But demand rarely is uniform and completely predictable, and stocks are not always replenished on time. That is why safety stocks are needed. Their function is to reduce the risk of stock-outs due to unexpected demand or late resupply.

### Lead Times

The lead time is the length of time between reordering and delivery of a product. This must be factored in when minimum stock is calculated. For example, if the lead time is four weeks and a recipe requires 20 units per week in inventory, then reordering must take place before the minimum inventory falls below 80 units. If replenishment of inventory does not come in time to meet customer demand, revenues and ultimately profits will suffer.

### Reorder Points

The inventory level that triggers the resupply process is called the reorder point. If everything were certain, then the reorder point would equal the normal usage during the normal lead time. But because of uncertainties in both usage and lead time, the reorder point (ROP) is equal to the safety stock (S) plus the demand during the normal lead time (DNLT). The equation looks like this:

$$ROP = S + DNLT$$

If a reorder point is based on a safety stock of 129 units and an average demand of the normal lead time of 237 units; then, the ROP is equal to 466 units.

## Hospitality Point-of-Sale System (POS)

A good computerized POS system is important; it can save you time, money and headaches. POS automation improves consistency, and accountability. It gives you powerful tools to monitor and manage the day-to-day operations of your restaurant. The right POS system allows you to accomplish more with less effort, improving customer service and net profits. Here are some areas that affect this small net profit portion of a restaurant dollar and that a POS can help with.

• Forgotten items: Lack of information on true food costs.
• Incorrect prices: Lack of control on sales.
• Forgotten charges: Lack of inventory control.
• Overages & shortages: Lack of control over voids.
• Cost of manual bookkeeping: Temptation/theft.

On the positive side, a good POS system affords you safeguards against common restaurant profit drains. POS automation can enable you to track inventory with greater precision, improving inventory control and allowing you to allocate funds to inventory when needed. POS can improve employee productivity and customer service by streamlining the order-entry process, allowing staff to accomplish more in the same amount of time, freeing them to spend more time attending to your customers. New employee training can be greatly streamlined as well. POS automation can help your back office, providing real-time information. With a POS system, you hopefully spend less time in the office and more time out on the floor with your customers and your staff, watching your business and profits grow.

On the negative side, POS systems can be expensive to purchase. The up-front costs for the basic package can be steep. Once you get the package you might have to invest in additional modules that you did not count on. For example, you may have to buy a nutrition costing module at a later date, which could cost as much as the primary software package or system. POS requires training for you, as the employer, and for your employees. POS can be expensive to maintain, in software upgrades and system upgrades.

There are hundreds of POS system developers to choose from, and there are many system configurations. Before you invest time in even investigating a system, be sure you know enough about your record keeping system to know what to look for, and what questions to ask. If you don't, you may wind up buying a system that will require you to invest hundreds of hours of training just to find out that the system does not meet your needs.

## Features of POS

Here is a sample list of features provided by POS software:

### Inventory

- Automatically removes used ingredients from stock.
- Uses perpetual inventory control system or merely adjusts to physical counts.
- Calculates costed stock on hand. There are many different costing methods, including: Actual cost, last cost, average cost, standard cost, First-In-First-Out (FIFO) and Last-In-Last-Out (LIFO).
- Allows for entering or importing of daily production and/or shipments and usage.
- Prints pick lists for ingredient requirements.
- Automatically adds finished production to stock and removes shipped products from stock.
- Inventory aging - identifies expired and old ingredients from stock.
- Generates shortage lists and reorder lists.
- Tracks vendor quotes.

### Recipe/Formula Costing Software

- Calculates complete product costs, including labor.
- Calculates gross margins, or lets the software calculate what your selling price should be in order to make your desired profit.
- Includes a database of approximately 4,000 common ingredients.
- Easily adds an unlimited number of other ingredients.
- Installs optional libraries of brand name ingredients.
- Prints NLEA Compliant Nutrition Labels.

## Operations Tips

### Tips for Controlling Food Costs and Handling & Storage

- When receiving be sure to examine all produce deliveries for bad product and return substandard products.
- Rotate your dry and refrigerated storage areas regularly to reduce spoilage and spills.
- Code-date, rotate and store, in sealed plastic, all freezer products to reduce spoilage and freezer burn.

- Store all refrigerated food in plastic or metal containers with lids; avoid using foil and plastic wrap.
- Donate edible, unsold food products to a local food distribution center or food bank.
- Adjust quantity or frequency of inventory shipments to minimize waste due to spoilage and dehydration.
- Use daily production charts to minimize over-prepping and unnecessary waste.
- Store produce far from the condenser to prevent freezing.
- Thaw frozen food in the refrigerator. It will help to avoid running water continuously over frozen foods such as shellfish.
- Inspect trimmings from food prep for composting. Also include coffee-grounds and citrus rinds from the bar.
- Use vegetable, fish, and meat trimmings in stock and other food preparation.
- Render used oil and check to see if the renderer takes meat bones.
- Resize portions and offer smaller plates if you find leftovers a pattern.
- Have servers encourage guests to take home leftovers.
- Buy shelf-stable prepared foods.
- Use health department approved, refillable dispensers rather than single serving packets (e.g.; butter, jam, dairy, sugars).
- If you purchase prepared mayonnaise, dressings etc., buy in larger quantities and store in plastic containers with tight-fitting lids.
- Consider buying some pre-trimmed produce to avoid prep waste, particularly when costs are equal to your bulk purchase and labor costs.
- If you use three or more cases of eggs per week, consider buying them shelled in bulk. This will increase yield and will eliminate broken eggs in the cooler and having to dispose of shells and boxes. Don't purchase eggs in polystyrene boxes.
- Serve beverages from a beverage gun or dispenser, and buy bar mixes in concentrate, and milk in 5-gallon dispenser boxes. Some jurisdictions have recycling for these aseptic boxes (labeled as Tetra Pac).
- Assign kitchen staff their own waste container. At the end of the shift, measure what they throw away.

## Maintenance Tips

- Develop a daily and weekly cleaning and maintenance program for all equipment. When purchasing new equipment, ensure the distributor has shown kitchen staff how to clean and maintain the equipment. Have equipment serviced by a maintenance and repair company to avoid costly repairs.

- Keep oven equipment calibrated.
- Clean fryers and filter oil frequently. Carbon deposits from food at the bottom of the fryer lengthen heating time. Use a test kit from a grocery distributor to determine when to change your oil.
- In cases where you use more than one deep fryer, specify a particular fryer for the product that is high in deposits. Change this oil more frequently.
- Reduce China breakage by placing rubber mats around the bus and dishwashing areas. Ceramic and container glass are not recyclable, and if found in great enough quantities in your recycling, will contaminate the load, forcing the recycler to haul it as garbage, typically at a higher rate.
- Create incentives for staff to reduce breakage.
- Ask staff to use reusable drink cups for their beverages if you have staff dining areas where disposables are used. Provide these ceramic or plastic cups for on-site use as well as their commute in to work.
- Manually compact trash in garbage cans and empty only when full.
- Consider purchasing a garbage compactor to reduce volume and check with hauler to determine its effect on pricing of services.
- Standardize your packaging to minimize use (durable storage containers which stack).
- Purchase gold or hemp coffee filters to minimize bleached paper coffee filter disposal.

### Recycling

- Compost your pre-consumer vegetative waste, coffee grounds and citrus peels.
- Establish a program where most items are capable of being recycled or reused. Check with local recycling companies for a recyclable commodities list and try to recycle cardboard, waxed cardboard (for composting), all paper (no carbon paper, glue or plastic envelope windows), glass, aluminum, tin (including clean tin foil), steel, #1 and #2 plastics, and in some jurisdictions, plastic wrap.
- Donate or exchange items which you no longer need or use. Check with your local materials exchange and non-profits for a ready taker.
- List contaminants that can ruin recycling efforts: ceramics, light bulbs, drink glasses, and pitchers.
- Reuse retired linens and uniforms as rags or donate them. They can be re-sewn for other uses.

# Safety

*It is better to be safe than sorry.*
*- Anonymous*

This chapter deals with food safety and employee safety. Although technically part of operations, we wanted this topic to have its own area in order to stress the importance. Here you will find procedures to help you draft a food-safety program, and descriptions of OSHA (Occupational Safety and Health Administration) online expert advisors, which will help you setup your business safety manuals.

## Food Safety

Many cities and counties require that your employees complete a food-safety certification course. These courses are usually available through the government certifying agency or third party. This is a requirement that you will want to investigate early in your planning process. Contact the local health department for specific details in your area.

The U. S. Food and Drug Administration oversees food processing. It has developed food safety guidelines for manufacturers and restaurants.

## HACCP

H.A.C.C.P. - Pronounced *has-sip,* is an acronym that stands for Hazard Analysis Critical Control Points. The goal of the program is to have critical check points across all levels of food processing and preparation. This is accomplished when a hazard analysis, based on anticipated hazards, is completed.

For years industry and regulators have been exploring use of the HACCP principles in restaurants, grocery stores, and other retail food establishments. During that time, much has been learned about how these principles can be used in the varied operations, collectively referred to as retail food establishments. Most of this exploration has focused on the question of how to stay true to the definitions of HACCP and still make the principles useful to an industry that encompasses the broadest range of conditions.

Despite this diversity and range of conditions, those involved have discovered that the HACCP principles are useful tools for managing food safety. Over time HACCP applications have been slightly modified to better fit retail food establishments.

### HACCP Background

HACCP is a common sense technique to control food-safety hazards. It is a preventive system of hazard control rather than a reactive one. Food establishments can use it to ensure safer food products for consumers. It is not a zero-risk system, but is designed to minimize the risk of food-safety hazards. HACCP is not a stand alone program but is one part of a larger system of control procedures that must be in place in order for HACCP to function effectively.

*Download* an Ebook about how to develop your HACCP plan from the Web site.

The success of a HACCP program is dependent upon both people and facilities. Management and employees must be properly motivated and trained if a HACCP program is to successfully reduce the risk of food-borne illness. Education and training in the principles of food safety and management commitment to the implementation of a HACCP system are critical and must be continuously reinforced. Instilling food-worker commitment and dealing with problems such as high employee turnover and communication barriers must be considered when designing a HACCP plan.

Successful implementation of a HACCP plan is also dependent upon the design and performance of facilities and equipment. The likelihood of the occurrence of a hazard in a finished product is influenced by facility and equipment design, construction, and installation, which play a key role in any preventive strategy.

## Risks Associated with Foods

According to the United States Food Code:

"Foodborne illness in the United States is a major cause of personal distress, preventable death, and avoidable economic burden. In 1994, the Council for Agricultural Science and Technology estimated that millions of people become ill from microorganisms in food, resulting in as many as 9,000 needless deaths every year... The Centers for Disease Control and Prevention (CDC) have consistently stated that where reported food-borne outbreaks were caused by mishandling of food, most of the time the mishandling occurred within the retail segment of the food industry. where ready-to-eat food is prepared and provided to the public for consumption."

Because many foods are agricultural products and have started their journey to your door as animals and plants, raised in the environment, they may contain microscopic organisms. Many foods contain nutrients that make them a place where microorganisms can live and even grow. Some of these organisms are pathogens, which means that under the right conditions and in the right numbers, they can make someone who eats them ill. Raw animal foods such as meat, poultry, fish, and eggs often carry bacteria, viruses, or parasites that can be harmful to humans. Because foods are from the environment, they can also contain objects such as stones that could cause injury. Food may be contaminated naturally, for example from the soil in which it is grown or because of harvest, storage, or transportation practices. Some foods undergo further processing and at times, despite best efforts, become contaminated. These inherent hazards, along with the hazards that may occur in your establishment, such as metal fragments from grinding, can lead to injury, illness, or death. Hazards include:

Biological concerns, such as:

• Bacterial, parasitic, or viral contamination.
• Bacterial growth.
• Bacterial, parasitic, or viral survival.
• Bacterial toxin production.
• Bacterial, parasitic, or viral cross-contamination.

Physical objects:

• Stones.
• Glass.
• Metal fragments.
• Packaging materials.

Chemical contamination:

• Nonfood-grade lubricants.
• Cleaning compounds.
• Food additives.
• Insecticides.

In a report from CDC titled, *Surveillance for Foodborne-Disease Outbreaks - United States, 1988-1992*, it is clear that bacterial agents are the leading cause of laboratory-confirmed outbreaks and that the main reasons for the outbreaks are:

• Improper holding temperatures,
• Poor personal hygiene,
• Improper cooking temperatures,
• Foods from unsafe sources, and
• Contaminated equipment.

## Using HACCP Principles

The goal in applying the HACCP principles at the retail level is to have managers and owners of establishments voluntarily take purposeful actions to ensure a safe outcome. Managing for food safety must be as fully integrated into your operations just as those actions that you might take to open in the morning, ensure a profit and manage cash flow, over-see personnel, or any other aspect of your business. Putting in place an active, ongoing system, made up of actions intended to create the desired outcome, is the only way to improve food safety. Application of the HACCP principles provides one system that can meet that criterion.

The HACCP principles, combined with a good set of Standard Operating Procedures (SOPs) and a sound training program, can be the most impor-tant part of a food-safety management system. The HACCP plan that you are going to develop is your plan. You may seek assistance from others such as your regulatory authority or an outside consultant, but the design, implementation, and success of the plan rests with you.

## The HACCP System Seven Principles

**1. Perform a Hazard Analysis.** This first principle is about under-standing your operation and determining what hazards are likely to occur. This usually involves defining the operational steps that you take as food enters and moves through your business. At this point, you will also try to understand how the people, equipment, methods, and foods all affect each other.

**2. Decide on the Critical Control Points (CCPs).** Which of the operational steps identified in principle #1 are critical to a safe outcome? Where can a hazard be prevented, eliminated, or reduced to an acceptable level? Which actions positively, absolutely, have to happen right? Is there a later step that will prevent, reduce, or eliminate the hazard? It is impor-tant to know that not all steps are CCPs. Generally, there are only a few CCPs in each process.

**3. Determine the Critical Limits.** Each CCP must have boundaries that define safety. How will you know when the CCPs are under control? What are the regulatory standards? What will you measure against? Critical limits are the measurements that define safety and can usually be found in the Food Code. For example, for cooking hamburgers, the Food Code sets the critical limits at 155°F for 15 seconds. When critical limits are not met, it could mean that the food is not safe.

**4. Establish Procedures to Monitor CCPs.** Once you have decided which operational steps are critical and have set the critical limits, someone needs to keep track of the CCPs in the flow of foods through your operation. Monitoring involves finding a way to see that the CCPs are kept under control and within the critical limits.

**5. Establish Corrective Actions.** What will you do when things go wrong? When monitoring your CCPs you will occasionally find an operational step that is outside of your critical limits. You need to plan ahead and decide what your actions will be, communicate those to your employees, and train them in those decisions. This preventive approach is at the heart of HACCP. Problems will arise. You need to find them and correct them before they can cause someone to become ill or injured.

**6. Establish Verification Procedures.** This principle is all about making sure that the whole system is in place and working. You will want to periodically make observations, calibrate equipment and temperature measuring devices, review records/actions, and discuss procedures with your employees. All of these activities will be for the purpose of ensuring that your system is real and checking to see if it needs to be modified or improved. Verification may also be conducted from the outside, such as by the regulatory authority or a third party.

**7. Establish a Record Keeping System.** There are certain written records or kinds of documentation that will be needed in order to verify that the system is working. Refer to the following table for examples of simplified records. These records will normally involve the HACCP plan, itself, and your monitoring activities and serve to document the fact that you really do have an on-going system in place. Record keeping should be as simple as possible in order to make it more likely that employees will have the time to keep the necessary records.

## Injury and Illness Prevention

Some states may require you, as an employer, to establish, implement and maintain a written Injury and Illness Prevention (IIP) Program. You can adapt this model to use in your store. Simply fill in the blanks and edit.

A copy of the program must be maintained at each worksite or at a central worksite if the employer has non-fixed worksites. The requirements for establishing, implementing, and maintaining an effective written Injury and Illness Prevention Program are:

- Responsibility.
- Compliance.
- Communication.
- Hazard assessment.
- Accident/exposure investigation.
- Hazard correction.
- Training and instruction.
- Record keeping.

This is a model program has been prepared for use by employers in industries which have been determined by OSHA to be non-high hazard. You are not required to use this program. However, any employer in an industry which has been determined by OSHA as being non-high hazard who adopts, posts, and implements this model program in good faith is not subject to assessment of a civil penalty.

Proper use of this model program requires that the IIP Program administrator of your establishment carefully reviews the requirements for each of the eight IIP Program elements, fills in the appropriate blank spaces and checks those items that are applicable to your workplace. The record keeping section requires that the IIP Program administrator select and implement the category appropriate for your establishment. Sample forms for hazard assessment and correction, accident/exposure investigation, and worker training and instruction are provided with this model program.

This model program must be maintained by the employer in order to be effective. The model program is a fill-in-the-blank program that you can adapt for use in your restaurant.

*See the online Safety eTools at the Web site.*

## Responsibility

The Injury and Illness Prevention (IIP) Program administrator,

_____

*Program Administrator*

has the authority and the responsibility for implementing and maintaining this IIP Program for

_____

*Establishment Name*

Managers and supervisors are responsible for implementing and maintaining the IIP Program in their work areas and for answering worker questions about the IIP Program. A copy of this IIP Program is available from each manager and supervisor.

## Compliance

All workers, including managers and supervisors, are responsible for complying with safe and healthful work practices. Our system of ensuring that all workers comply with these practices include one or more of the following practices:

• Informing workers of the provisions of our IIP Program.
• Evaluating the safety performance of all workers.
• Recognizing employees who perform safe and healthful work practices.
• Providing training to workers whose safety performance is deficient.
• Disciplining workers for failure to comply with safe work practices.

## Communication

All managers and supervisors are responsible for communicating with all workers about occupational safety and health in a form readily understandable by all workers. Our communication system encourages all workers to inform their managers and supervisors about workplace hazards without fear of reprisal.

Our communication system includes one or more of the following checked items:

- New worker orientation including a discussion of safety and health policies and procedures.
- Review of our IIP Program.
- Training programs.
- Regularly scheduled safety meetings.
- Posted or distributed safety information.
- A system for workers to anonymously inform management about workplace hazards.
- Our establishment has less than ten employees and communicates with and instructs employees orally about general safe work practices and hazards unique to each employee's job assignment.

## Hazard Assessment

Periodic inspections to identify and evaluate workplace hazards shall be performed by a competent observer in the following areas of our workplace: *(List workplace hazards.)*

_____

_____

_____

Periodic inspections are performed according to the following schedule:

- When we initially established our IIP Program;
- When new substances, processes, procedures or equipment which present potential new hazards are introduced into our workplace;
- When new, previously unidentified hazards are recognized;
- When occupational injuries and illnesses occur; and
- Whenever workplace conditions warrant an inspection.

## Accident Exposure and Investigations

Procedures for investigating workplace accidents and hazardous substance exposures include:

- Interviewing injured workers and witnesses.
- Examining the workplace for factors associated with the accident/exposure.

- Determining the cause of the accident/exposure.
- Taking corrective action to prevent the accident/exposure from reoccurring; and recording the findings and actions taken.

## Hazard Correction

Unsafe or unhealthy work conditions, practices or procedures shall be corrected in a timely manner based on the severity of the hazards. Hazards shall be corrected according to the following procedures:

- When observed or discovered; and
- When an imminent hazard exists which cannot be immediately abated without endangering employee(s) and/or property, we will remove all exposed workers from the area except those necessary to correct the existing condition. Workers who are required to correct the hazardous condition shall be provided with the necessary protection.

## Training and Instruction

All workers, including managers and supervisors, shall have training and instruction on general and job-specific safety and health practices. Training and instruction is provided:

- When the IIP Program is first established.
- To all new workers, except for construction workers who are provided training through a construction industry occupational safety and health training program approved by OSHA.
- To all workers given new job assignments for which training was not previously provided.
- Whenever new substances, processes, procedures or equipment are introduced to the workplace and represent a new hazard.
- Whenever the employer is made aware of a new or previously unrecognized hazard.
- To supervisors to familiarize them with the safety and health hazards to which workers under their immediate direction and control may be exposed.
- To all workers with respect to hazards specific to each employee's job assignment.

General workplace safety and health practices include, but are not limited to, the following:

- Implementation and maintenance of the IIP Program.
- Emergency action and fire prevention plan.
- Provisions for medical services and first aid including emergency procedures.
- Prevention of musculoskeletal disorders, including proper lifting techniques.
- Proper housekeeping, such as keeping stairways and aisles clear, work areas neat and orderly, and promptly cleaning up spills.
- Prohibiting horseplay, scuffling, or other acts that tend to adversely influence safety.
- Proper storage to prevent stacking goods in an unstable manner and storing goods against doors, exits, fire extinguishing equipment and electrical panels.
- Proper reporting of hazards and accidents to supervisors.
- Hazard communication, including worker awareness of potential chemical hazards, and proper labeling of containers.
- Proper storage and handling of toxic and hazardous substances including prohibiting eating or storing food and beverages in areas where they can become contaminated.

## Record Keeping

We have embraced one of the following categories as our record keeping policy. *(Choose one category.)*

### Category 1

Our establishment has twenty or more workers or has a workers' compensation experience modification rate of greater than 1.1 and is not on a designated low-hazard industry list. We have taken the following steps to implement and maintain our IIP Program:

- Records of hazard assessment inspections, including the person(s) conducting the inspection, the unsafe conditions and work practices that have been identified and the action taken to correct the identified unsafe conditions and work practices, are recorded on a hazard assessment and correction form; and

• Documentation of safety and health training for each worker, including the worker's name or other identifier, training dates, type(s) of training, and training providers are recorded on a worker training and instruction form.

Inspection records and training documentation will be maintained:

• For one year, except for training records of employees who have worked for less than one year which are provided to the employee upon termination of employment; or
• Since we have less than ten workers, including managers and supervisors, we only maintain inspection records until the hazard is corrected and only maintain a log of instructions to workers with respect to worker job assignments when they are first hired or assigned new duties.

## Category 2

Our establishment has fewer than twenty workers and is not on a designated high-hazard industry list. We are also on a designated low-hazard industry list or have a workers' compensation experience modification rate of 1.1 or less, and have taken the following steps to implement and maintain our IIP Program:

• Records of hazard assessment inspections; and
• Documentation of safety and health training for each worker.

Inspection records and training documentation will be maintained according to the following checked schedule:

• For one year, except for training records of employees who have worked for less than one year which are provided to the employee upon termination of employment; or
• Since we have less than ten workers, including managers and supervisors, we maintain inspection records only until the hazard is corrected, and only maintain a log of instructions to workers with respect to worker- job assignments when they are first hired or assigned new duties.

## Category 3

We are a local governmental entity and we are not required to keep written records of the steps to implement and maintain our IIP Program.

# Hazard Assessment and Correction Form

Date of Inspection:_____

Person Conducting Inspection:

_____

Unsafe Condition or Work Practice:

_____

_____

Corrective Action Taken:

_____

_____

_____

_____

Unsafe Condition or Work Practice:

_____

_____

Corrective Action Taken:

_____

_____

_____

_____

Unsafe Condition or Work Practice:

_____

_____

Corrective Action Taken:

_____

_____

_____

_____

## Accident and Investigation Report

Date & Time of Accident: _____

Location: _____

Accident Description:

_____
_____
_____
_____
_____
_____

Workers Involved:

_____
_____
_____
_____
_____
_____

Preventive Action Recommendations:

_____
_____
_____
_____
_____
_____

Corrective Actions Taken:

_____
_____
_____
_____
_____
_____

Manager Responsible:_____

Date Completed: _____

# Employee Training and Instruction Record

Employee Name:_____
Start Date:_____
Employee Orientation Completion Date_____

## 1. HACCP Training

Date:_____
Trainer's Name:_____

## 2. Safety Training

Date:_____
Trainer's Name:_____

## 3. Equipment Operation and Maintenance Procedures

Date:_____
Trainer's Name:_____

## 4. Injury and Illness Prevention Procedures

Date:_____
Trainer's Name:_____

## 5. Hazard Communication Procedures

Date:_____
Trainer's Name:_____

## 6. Fire Safety Procedures

Date:_____
Trainer's Name:_____

## Fire Safety

You will need to draft a fire safety program and train all your employees in its procedures. This must include a fire egress plan, information regarding fire extinquishers in your restaurant, and information about halon gas fire extinguishers for your cooking hood and grill.

OSHA has developed an online *Fire Safety Advisor*, an interactive expert software program. It will help you understand and apply OSHA's fire safety related standards. It addresses OSHA's general industry standards for fire safety and emergency evacuation. It also addresses OSHA standards for firefighting, fire suppression and fire detection systems and equipment.

This expert software will interview you about your building, work practices, and policies at the facility, to determine whether and how OSHA's fire safety standards may apply.

The Fire Safety Advisor will:

• Ask you about workplace conditions, practices, and policies.
• Analyzes your answers with expert decision-logic.
• Alert you to fire safety hazards.
• Point out applicable OSHA standards.
• Tell you what aspects of these standards apply to your situation.
• Help you conduct detailed compliance reviews.
• Help you write customized "Emergency Action Plans" and "Fire Prevention Plans".
• Give you reformatted and very readable copy of the regulations, and other help.

*See more details about the online expert systems in Chapter 13 and at the Web site.*

## General Safety

OSHA also has developed an expert system called, *The eLaws Safety and Health Advisor Online*. It will help you review and evaluate key aspects of your Safety and Health Program, if you have one. If you do not have one, it could help you think about elements of a good program. It is straightforward and very easy to use.

This Safety and Health Program Evaluation software:

• Interviews users to evaluate their establishments safety and health programs.
• Identifies areas that need improvement, and points you toward higher levels of quality.
• Acknowledges good program elements.
• Tells users with successful program elements about the exemplary programs.
• Writes you a report on your based on your input and conclusions.
• Includes a model program and related program development information.

By using the software advisors mentioned above, you will save countless hours, and at the same time, you can be assured that you will be in compliance with government requirements in regard to safety.

## Chapter Notes

# Taxes & Insurance

*Question: Define Taxes, Answer: Legal Extortion*
*Question: Define Extortion, Answer: Taxes*
*- Robin Hood*

This chapter will outline what you will need to know about taxes and insurance. You will need to know what taxes you need to collect and report to appropriate government agencies, and what insurance you will need as a restaurant owner.

# Taxes & Insurance

The old adage, "death & taxes", applies to business. There is a myriad of taxes that you will be responsible for as a business owner. Taxes are evoked at all levels of government, from federal down through the local level. Permits will be also required. From building permits, health permits, to fire permits. Finally, there are many types of insurance that you will need in order to operate your business. Most of these are mandatory as they are dictated by government agencies and/or your landlord.

Your accountant will be familiar with the different forms that you will have to file. The person or service doing your payroll will be familiar with the forms required for payroll deductions and taxes. The tax laws in this chapter can be complex, and they are forever changing. Therefore always seek professional advice from an accountant or tax expert, when in doubt or it you have specific questions.

***TIP***

*You can get IRS forms at their Web site:*
***www.irs.gov***

## Taxes

### Employer Tax Requirements

If you hire employees, you will have to comply with various legal requirements and know about state and federal forms and filing procedures. It may be advantageous to use the services of an accounting or business counseling firm, to both complete and file the forms for you, or to teach you how to do it. While the process appears complex, many business owners handle it easily. Above all, accurate record keeping is essential for timely and correct filing of employer tax.

### Employer Identification Number

All employers, corporations and partnerships are required to obtain a federal employer identification number (EIN). The EIN identifies your business's tax accounts on all federal and state tax forms. A sole proprietor without employees does not need to obtain an EIN and may use his or her Social Security number instead.

To apply for your federal EIN, file Form SS-4, which you can obtain from an IRS or Social Security office. No fee is required. Allow several weeks for your identification numbers to be mailed. For more information call 1-800-829-1040.

## Employees and Independent Contractors

Businesses sometimes prefer to hire a person as an independent contractor because the nature or duration of the work does not justify hiring a person as an employee.

If a business hires and pays an independent contractor $600 or more during the year, the business is required to report this information to the IRS using Form 1099. A business is not required to withhold or pay employer taxes for monies it pays an independent contractor. The independent contractor is responsible for reporting his or her income and paying taxes. The distinction between an employee and an independent contractor is important to understand because the IRS may assess taxes and penalties if a worker is improperly treated as a contractor instead of as an employee. The difference depends on the working relationship between the employer and the person performing services.

Independent contractors, generally, are persons who offer their services to the general public. The general rule is that a person is an independent contractor if the employer has the right to control or direct the result of the work but not the methods or means of accomplishing the work. Independent contractors generally supply their own tools, work at times and places of their choosing, and cannot be discharged by the employer. A written contract for work may help define these facts.

In contrast, in an employer-employee relationship the employer supplies tools and a place to work, has the right to fire the employee, and generally controls the means of work.

There are exceptions to these general rules and sometimes it may be difficult to know the correct decision. Check with your accountant or tax professional if you are unsure. If the IRS concludes that an employer has no reasonable basis for treating a worker as an independent contractor, the employer may be liable for back payroll taxes for the worker.

## Employer Tax Withholding

As an employer, the law requires you to withhold federal and state income taxes and Social Security (FICA) taxes from the earnings of each of your employees. In addition, the business is required to make payments from its own funds to Social Security for each employee.

The amount of income and Social Security taxes to be withheld and paid for each employee will vary depending on the rate of pay, marital status, and number of exemptions claimed by the employee on the Form W-4 described below. If you are preparing employer tax returns yourself, be sure that you have the most recent withholding tax tables since these tables change frequently due to changes in the tax law.

Federal withholding and Social Security taxes are filed four times a year on Form 941. Small businesses make payments monthly; large businesses make payments twice a week. For this purpose, a small business is one which reported $50,000 or less in payroll taxes the prior year. The payments are made via deposits to a bank using Coupon 8109.

Each employee must complete and return to you a federal Form W-4 at the beginning of his or her employment and when he or she wishes to change it. The W-4 indicates the number of exemptions which the employee claims so that you can properly determine withholding amounts during the year.

If you are a sole proprietor or a partner in a partnership, you are not considered an employee and are not subject to withholding. In lieu of withholding, you may be required to make quarterly estimated tax payments if withholding from your other income, such as salary from another job, is not enough.

If your business is incorporated, you as the owner are automatically an employee and are subject to withholding on any salary that the corporation pays you. Therefore, you would not have to file estimated tax returns as an individual. However the corporation may be required to make estimated tax payments on corporate income, using Form 1120-W.

## Unemployment Tax

The federal government requires employers to pay an unemployment tax that is based on an employee's wages. The Federal Unemployment Tax (FUTA) is filed on federal Form 940. The FUTA tax must be paid at least annually by January 31 of the following year or quarterly on Coupon 8109 if a higher payroll requires it.

Unemployment insurance offers workers protection from loss of earnings while partially or completely laid off from their jobs through no fault of their own. Most states have an unemployment tax that is paid for entirely by the employer. The tax is usually figured as a percentage of the employer's total payroll. You will need to check with your state to get specific details about how this tax is dealt with in your state.

## Employment Eligibility

Under the Immigration Reform and Control Act of 1986, all new employees must verify with their employer their eligibility to work. New employees must be American citizens or aliens who are authorized to work in this country.

As an employer, you must verify employment eligibility of anyone hired after November 6, 1986, and complete and retain a one-page Employment Eligibility Verification (Form I-9). The Immigration and Naturalization Service publishes a Handbook For Employers, Form M-274, which explains the law and how to comply. For more information, call the Immigration & Naturalization Service at 1-800-357-2099. Your state may also have specific forms that may need to be filed.

## Employee Tips and Taxes

The IRS requires that all employee tips - an acronym that means to insure proper service - be monitored and reported as part of your employees income.

All tips your employees receive are income and are subject to federal income tax. Each employee must include as gross income all tips he or she receives directly from customers, tips from charge customers that are paid to them by you, their employer, and your share of any tips that he or she receives under a tip-splitting or tip-pooling arrangement. The value of non-cash tips, such as tickets, passes, or other items of value are also income and subject to tax.

Employees are required to keep records regarding tips. They are to:

• Keep a daily tip record.
• Report tips to you, their employer.
• Report all tips on their income tax return.

Employees must report tip income on Form 4070, Employee's Report of Tips to Employer, or on a similar statement. This report is due on the 10th day of the month after the month the tips are received. This statement must be signed by the employee and must show the following:

- The employee's name, address, and SSN.
- Your name and address.
- The month or period the report covers.
- The total tips received.
- No report is required from an employee for months when tips are less than $20.

Both Forms 4070 and 4070-A, Employee's Daily Record of Tips, are included in Publication 1244, Employee's Daily Record of Tips and Report to Employer.

Employers must collect income tax, employee Social Security tax and employee Medicare tax on tips reported by employees. You can collect these taxes from an employee's wages or from other funds he or she makes available.

As an employer, you must ensure that the total tip income reported to you during any pay period is, at a minimum, equal to 8% of your total receipts for that period. In calculating 8% of total receipts, you do not include nonallocable receipts. Nonallocable receipts are defined as receipts for carry-out sales and receipts with an added service charge of 10% or more.

When the total reported to you is less than 8%, you must allocate the difference between the actual tip income reported and 8% of gross receipts. There are three methods for allocating tip income:

- Gross receipt method.
- Hours worked method.
- Good faith agreement.

Employers can request a lower rate (but not lower than 2%) for tip allocation purposes by submitting an application to the IRS. Detailed instructions for computing allocation of tips, reporting allocated tips to employees, and for requesting a lower rate can be found in the Instructions for Form 8027.

Note: The amount shown as allocated tip income is for information purposes only. You are not required to withhold income or Social Security taxes on the allocated tip income. The amount of tip income allocated to each employee is shown in box 8 of their Form W-2.

Employers who operate large food or beverage establishments must file Form 8027 to report employee tip income. A large food or beverage establishment is defined as business where all of the following apply:

• Food or beverage is provided for consumption on the premises.
• Tipping is a customary practice.
• More than 10 employees, who worked more than 80 hours, were normally employed on a typical business day during the preceding calendar year.

A worksheet for determining whether a business meets the criteria listed above is included in the Instructions for Form 8027.

## Inventory Taxes and Valuation

The government taxes inventory. It is important for you to use methods of inventory valuation to your advantage. You cannot simply expense inventory at the end of your accounting period, which is usually annual for sole proprietorships. Restaurant managers must reduce the amount paid for inventory purchases by the value of the inventory at the end of the year. For example, if you paid $15,000 for inventory in one year, and your inventory value at the end of that year was $10,000, you would be able to deduct $5,000 for total purchases. The remainder of the inventory would be taxable as a current asset.

The First-In, First-Out (FIFO), method of valuing inventory is based on the assumption that items in the beginning inventory and the goods purchased in the early part of the accounting period are the first to be sold. Therefore, the foods purchased last are the last to be sold and are in the ending inventory. This does not mean that the goods purchased first were actually sold first, but inventory valuation is determined on that basis.

The Last-In, First-Out, (LIFO) method of valuing inventory assumes that goods purchased last are the ones sold first. Using this method, we can assume that the goods in the beginning inventory, or those purchased early in the accounting period, will be sold last, and therefore make up the ending inventory.

The method that you choose to value your inventory is important for tax planning. For example, if the economy is in an inflationary trend, a change to LIFO will save taxes for your store by allowing a loss deduction for the price increases of your inventory throughout the year.

## Income Tax

Individuals that are part of a sole proprietorship or partnerships are not generally paid as employees. No income tax is withheld from money that they take out of the business. They must estimate their tax liability each year and then pay in quarterly installments throughout the year. At the end of the year thy must file an income tax return as an individual and pay any taxes due on the profits earned in the business for that year.

Business organized as a corporation has a different income tax scenario. Owners in a corporation will generally be paid a salary just like any other employee. Because a corporation legally acts as an individual, any profits it makes will accrue to itself. Therefore, corporations must file a tax return and the owners must file their own tax returns.

Corporations can file their tax returns on a calendar or fiscal year basis. A calender year is a typical year, from January to December. A fiscal year can end in any month. This can have an advantage for many business owners because they can end their tax year in any month that they choose.

## Sales Taxes

As a business owner, the government will want you to record, monitor, and collect sales taxes. Sales taxes are usually computed as a percentage of the sale. For example, 10% sales tax on a hamburger costing $3.00 would be 0.30. Sales taxes vary from state to state. Many are paid to the state on a monthly basis and are computed as a percentage of your gross taxable sales. You will need to check with the state that your business is located in for specific details about sales taxes.

## Sellers Permit

In order to protect businesses from being double taxed on the items that they purchase for resale, sellers permits are issued. These are generally issued by states that collect sales taxes (not all states collect them). Once you obtain your sellers permit, you can then purchase items tax exempt from your suppliers. You will be required to provide your permit number to these suppliers because this is a government requirement.

Some states mandate that sales taxes be estimated and paid in advance. For example, if you project $15,000 in gross taxable sales at the start of your business, and the sales tax is 10%, you will be required to advance deposit $1,500 in a tax account before the state will issue you a sellers permit.

## Insurance

Going into business is a risk. To succeed in business, the many potential risks must be managed, i.e., reduced and controlled. One of the methods of controlling risks is with insurance. For the small firm the most common risks are:

• Business fraud and theft.
• Fire.
• Legal liability - injury to customers or employees, defective merchandise, etc.
• Business interruptions.
• Death or loss of key personnel.
• Death or loss of owner or partner.
• Violent weather -- hurricanes, floods, etc.
• Damage to or loss of vehicles.

If a business has even one employee, workers' compensation insurance is mandatory. In several states, if a business has five or more employees, health insurance is required. When applying for a loan, banks may require certain types of insurance, depending on the nature of the business and the type of loan.

Each business will have its own particular insurance needs. At business start-up, funds to purchase insurance may be limited. Nevertheless, insurance must be investigated and that which is essential must be purchased.

The general categories of insurance are:

- Property.
- Automobile and vehicular.
- General liability.
- Product liability.
- Group life and health.
- Fidelity and surety.
- Workers' compensation.

Before purchasing insurance, find out which types are required, how you can reduce the cost of coverage, and which risks you can afford to cover yourself. Also, you must decide which kind of risk protection will work best and be most economical for you. Here are some typical *specific* types of coverage:

- Fire and property insurance - covers fire losses, vandalism, and weather related damage.
- Boiler Insurance - covers damage caused by building boiler.
- Plate glass insurance - covers window breakage.
- Burglary insurance - covers forced entry and/or theft of merchandise or cash.
- Consequential loss insurance - covers loss of revenues due to catastrophe or act of God.
- Earthquake insurance - covers specific damage caused by an earthquake.
- Fidelity bonding - covers theft or embezzlement by employee.
- Public liability insurance - covers injuries to the public. For example, falls on store premises.
- Product liability insurance - covers injury to customers that may come from products or supplies purchased by the company.
- Life insurance - covers partners, owners, and employees.

Assign priorities. Cover your largest loss exposure first; the less severe as your budget permits.

Usually the life savings of a small business owner are invested in the business and often homes are used to secure notes. What happens when the owner dies? Does the business close? Does the family of the owner have to stand by and watch savings and other assets go down the drain?

You can protect both your business and your family with business life insurance. Consult your agent so that a business life insurance policy is tailored to fit the needs of your family and your business. A suitable business life insurance program can:

- Ensure immediate funds to meet taxes, debts, and administrative expenses.
- Provide income for heirs.
- Equitably distribute the property value to heirs.
- Enable your executor or administrator to dispose of your business to the best advantage if your family is not taking over.
- Put your family on a sound financial basis if the family is assuming the operation of the business.
- Stabilize the credit of the business.
- Help maintain good employee relations by eliminating uncertainties and hazards.
- If the business is a partnership, provide a prearranged plan for the orderly and equitable dissolution of the partnership and the opportunity for surviving partners to buy out the heirs.
- Provide funds to replace a key employee or train another if the key employee leaves, becomes ill, or dies. This is called "Key Employee" insurance.

## Worker's Compensation Insurance

Any employer who has three or more regular employees is required to furnish, at no cost to the employee, worker's compensation insurance; hence, this is really more like a tax. The insurance may be purchased through a private insurance company or the employer can apply to the Industrial Commission to obtain a certificate of self-insurance. The cost of the insurance varies by industry and occupation.

Worker's compensation insurance provides compensation and medical benefits to workers or their dependents if the workers become disabled or die from accidental injury or occupational disease due to their employment. Check with your state for specific insurance requirements.

Insurance is one area of your business where professional help is strongly recommended to obtain proper coverage at the best price. Help is readily available from local insurance agents and brokers, the best choice being one who writes insurance for other small businesses.

One way to determine which insurance agent is best for you is to ask other small business owners whom they use and what kind of service they receive. Your banker, accountant or attorney may also be able to recommend an agent or broker. Look in the yellow pages of the phone book under "Insurance" to find qualified agents.

# The Web Site

T his chapter explains some of the products and services that you will find at the web site, which accompanies this book. Many of the software programs are available as demos and some are free. To log on go to, *www.bizventures.com* and enter the purchase code: *rest101* in order to register.

## Instructions

Download the contents by right-clicking on the appropriate hyperlink and then select Save and navigate to your desired folder location on your hard drive. Note that many of the download files are in a ZIP file format; therefore, after downloading, unzip them to your desired folder. Also, you will need Microsoft Word and Excel in order to edit some of the files, as well as Adobe Acrobat Reader installed on your system to view the PDF files. If you do not have them installed on your system here are links you can go to: (If you leave the site to download these utility programs, you my have to log back on).

1. Open Office: A Microsoft Word and Excel compatible program you can install to edit document and spreadsheet files. Go to:

*www.openoffice.org*

2. Adobe Acrobat Reader: Used to view PDF files. Go to:

*www.adobe.com*

3. Winzip: Use this application for unzipping files. Go to:

*www.winzip.com*

## Core Business Planning

### Sample Business Plan

Here is a sample business plan that you can view/edit. These corresponds to the business plan in Chapter 4 of the book.

- Wrapbiz97.xls - This file is the financial spreadsheet. It contains a three year forecast, which include: Sales forecast, Profit and loss statements, balance sheets and cashflow statements. The spreadsheet also contains a loan calculator that will amortize payments. Follow the procedures contained within the spreadsheet. See page 4.3 in the book.

- Wrapequip.xls - This is the equipment list. This is part of the start-up cost schedule.

- WrapBizPlan.doc - This is the sample business plan in a Microsoft Word file.

- Floor_Plan.pdf - Sample store layout indexed to Wrapequip.xls, above.

- Wsmcomp.xls - Strength & weakness analysis spreadsheet.

*Download file: business_plan.zip*

## Customer Profile Development

Use these Excel spreadsheets to develop a bottom-up customer profile. The results can be compiled into a chart like the one on page 4.17 in the book.

*Download file: Customer_Profile.zip*

## Menu Sales Mix Analysis Spreadsheet

See page 10.14 in the book.

*Download file: menu.xls*

# Application Software

## Project Management Software

Open Work Bench is an open source project management tool designed to keep your project on track. What is a project?

A project could be opening a foodservice operation. We highly recommend that you use this kind of program from the very start of your endeavors because it will help budgeting and keep you on track. Open Workbench is an opensource program that will meet your planning needs After installing the program, open the file called, To Do List.rmp, which is a sample project for opening a restaurant that you can view/edit.

*Download file: openworkbench.zip*

## Employee Shift Scheduling Software

If you are running a multi-shift employee operation in food service, then Scheduling Employees for Windows is a must. This award winning shareware software program is a cinch to learn and will pay big dividends. Click the link do download the demo program.

*Download file: Employee_Scheduling.zip*

### Nutrition Analysis Software

Today's savvy consumer expects to have nutrition information included on the menu. Recipe Calc, a shareware program, helps you analyze the nutritional value of your recipes, meals, and daily food intake. It calculates total calories, calories from fat, the percentage of calories from fat, fat weight (in grams), cholesterol, carbohydrates, sodium, and protein. It displays this information in the standard nutrition facts label format, making it simple to interpret the data. A large database of common food ingredients is included in the program, and users can add ingredients to the database. With a simple click, email recipes. You can now save your recipes as Web pages. There is a larger ingredient database and interface enhancements. Click the link to download the demo program.

*Download file: recipecalc.zip*

## Occupational Safety and Health Administration (OSHA) Software Application Programs

Note: This section supersedes page 13.3 in your book. The Hazard Awarness and Saftey and Health sections have been replaced by the eLaws Safety and Health Advisor Online below. These expert systems used to available as stand along programs, which would run on your PC. However, the government has made these expert systems online, a huge advantage when trying to keep abreast of all the laws and updates.

### Safety Pays

Safety Pays is a tool developed by the Occupational Safety and Health Administration (OSHA) to assist employers in assessing the impact of occupational injuries and illnesses on their profitability. It uses a company's profit margin, the average costs of an injury or illness, and an indirect cost multiplier to project the amount of sales a company would need to generate in order to cover those costs.

Log on to the Web: (Online eTool)

*http://www.osha.gov/dcsp/smallbusiness/safetypays/index.html*

### Fire Safety

The Fire Safety Online Advisor program provides interactive expert help. It addresses OSHA's general industry standards for fire safety and emergency evacuation, and for fire fighting, fire suppression, and fire detection systems and equipment. The expert system asks you about building and business policies and practices. It asks follow-up questions based on your answers to prepare the guidance and write the customized plans you need.

Log on to the Web: (Online eTool)

*http://www.osha.gov/SLTC/etools/evacuation/expertsystem/default.htm*

### eLaws Safety and Health Advisor Online

This is an excellent starting point to access your government regulation requirements. Go online and take the advisor quiz in order to find out what you will be responsible for.

Log on to the Web: (Online eTool)

*http://www.dol.gov/elaws*

## PDF Documents

Here you will find various documents that will help you with OSHA inspections and assist with job-hazard analysis procedures that will become part of your operations manual.

### Manuals

• OSHA inspections.
• OSHA handbook for small business.
• Job hazard analysis.
• What to expect during OSHA's visit.

## Posters

Here you will find government informational posters that you will be required to post in your establishment.

- Job safety poster.
- Equal opportunity poster.
- Equal opportunity poster in Spanish.
- Employee polygraph protection act poster.
- Employee family medical leave act poster.
- Employee family medical leave act poster in Spanish.

*Download file: manuals_posters.zip*

## Ebooks

We have put together a series of electronic PDF books that you can download.

- How to Get aTtrademark.
- How to Get a Patent.
- Managing food safety guide: How to develop your HACCP food safety program.

*Download file: eBooks.zip*

# Appendix

This is the appendix. Here you will find a supplemental information, contact list, and bibliography.

## Associations and Magazines

**National Restaurant Association**
1200 17th St., NW   Washington, DC 20036
(202) 331-5900
www.restaurant.org

**Nation's Restaurant News**
425 Park Avenue
New York, NY 10022
(800) 944-4676
www.nrn.com

**Restaurant Business Magazine**
P.O. Box 1252
Skokie, IL 60076-9719
(847) 647-7987
http://www.restaurantbiz.com

**Restaurant Marketing**
307 West Jackson Ave.
Oxford, MS  38655
(800) 247-3881
www.restaurant-marketing.net

**Restaurants and Institutions Magazine**
2000 Clearwater Drive
Oak Brook, IL 60544-8809
Tel: (630) 288-8204
www.rimag.com

# Food Safety Links and Government Web Sites

**U.S. Agricultural Library**
www.nal.usda.gov

**Center for Food Safety and Applied Nutrition**
www.cfsan.fda.gov

**U.S. Department of Agriculture Food Safety and Inspection Service**
www.fsis.usda.gov

**The National Oceanic and Atmospheric Administration (NOAA)**
http://seafood.nmfs.noaa.gov

**Seafood Network Information Center**
http://seafood.ucdavis.edu/home.htm

**U.S. Small Business Administration**
www.sba.gov
www.business.gov

**U.S. Internal Revenue Service**
www.irs.gov

**U.S. Federal Trade Commission**
www.ftc.gov

**U.S. Department of Labor**
www.dol.gov

## Bibliography

*Business Buyer's Handbook*, by Jim Calkins. Published by Oak Tree Publishing, Claremont, California.

*Restaurant Purchasing: Principles and Practice*, by Hugh J. Kelly. Published by Chain Store Publishing Corporation, New York, New York.

*Fundamentals of Production/Operations Management*, by Harold E. Fearon. Published by West Publishing Company, Los Angeles, California.

*Principles of Accounting*, by Melvin Morgenstein. Published by HBJ Media Systems Corporation, New York, New York.

*Marketing*, by Carl McDaniel, Jr. Published by Harper & Row, New York, New York.

*Marketing Management: Strategy and Cases*, by Douglas J. Dalrymple. Published by John Wiley & Sons, New York, New York.

# Index

## Notes

# Notes

## Notes

# Notes

## Notes

## About the Author

*Paul Daniels was raised in southern California. He graduated in 1987 from California State University Long Beach with a Bachelor of Science in Marketing. He has been involved in restaurant and business consulting for the past 25 years. He currently works for Venture Marketing, a business media firm. When not researching and consulting, Paul enjoys writing songs and spending time with his family.*

*Never Quit.*